CO

TREES

Text by Dick Warner
Photographic Consultants
David and Jean Hosking

HarperCollins*Publishers*

HarperCollins*Publishers*
PO Box, Glasgow G4 0NB
First published 1995

Reprint 9 8 7 6 5 4 3 2 1

The copyright in the photographs belongs to the following photographers from the Frank Lane Picture Agency:

L. Batten 245b; R.F. Bird 228; B. Borrell 177, 178; H. D. Brandl 74; B. B. Casals 144; M. Clark 232; L. Colangeli/Panda 6; Dembinsky 56; P. Heard 83, 119; E. H. Herbert 102, 107, 163, 201, 234t, 235b; D. Hosking 95, 100, 218; E. & D. Hosking 22, 33, 42, 44, 51, 52, 57, 58, 66-7, 68, 69, 76, 79, 80, 82, 84, 87, 89, 92, 93, 96, 99, 104, 108-9, 121, 124, 125, 127, 129, 132, 133, 134, 135, 136, 138, 139, 145, 150, 151, 152, 153, 154, 159, 165, 168, 175, 180, 182, 183, 185, 194, 197, 198, 200, 202, 211, 220, 221, 223, 224, 226, 240b, 241t, 241b, 242b, 245t, 250b, 251b, 252; J. Hosking 174; J. Hutchings 115, 237b; Dick Jones 156, 208; M. Nimmo 25, 48, 49, 55, 60, 62, 63, 64, 77, 81, 86, 101, 122, 130, 141, 146, 147, 148, 149, 157, 164, 179, 181, 184, 188, 192, 205, 207, 210, 213, 222, 231, 234b, 239t 246b; P. Perry 41, 43, 233b; A. Petretti/Panda 186; F. Polking 71; W. Rohdich 18; I. Rose 215, 247t; M. Rose 65, 90, 98, 117, 123; R. Savelli/Panda 142, 143, 160, 171, 246t; Silvestris 45, 47, 54, 59, 61, 75, 78, 85, 91, 94, 105, 106, 110, 111, 113, 116, 118, 120, 128, 131, 137, 140, 155, 158, 167, 176, 189, 190, 193, 206, 209, 219, 225, 227, 229, 233t, 235t, 236b, 237t, 238t, 238b, 239b, 242t, 244t, 244b, 248b, 249t, 249b, 250t, 251t; Smith/Polunin 97, 103, 126, 161, 191; H. Smith 187, 212, 214, 216, 217; M. J. Thomas 53, 70, 196, 240t, 243b; J. Watkins 199; L. West 204; A. Wharton 8, 73, 114, 247b; A. Wilson 170; R. Wilmshurst 46, 166, 173, 236t, 243t; W. Wisniewski 169, 248t

ISBN 0 00470545 9

Typeset by TJ Graphics
Printed in Italy by Amadeus S.p.A.

CONTENTS

The species in this book are arranged in families. Many of these families are quite large and contain many plants which are not trees. Families are useful for identification purposes as, with some exceptions, trees in the same family look rather alike. The family name is given at the top of each page.

INTRODUCTION

This book describes over 180 species of tree, covering all those likely to be seen in Britain and Ireland, whether wild or cultivated. Colour photographs and concise descriptions provide all the information needed to identify them and learn something of their fascinating natural history.

Throughout the book technical and botanical terms have been replaced by simple English alternatives. For this reason the book has no glossary, but a section called Key words (p.39) explains some words and ideas which may be unfamiliar to the beginner. Other key words are highlighted in bold in this introduction.

Although this book is based on the trees found in Britain and Ireland it will be just as useful in other parts of northern Europe and covers many trees found in other temperate areas of the world and in southern Europe.

The natural history of trees

Some 400 million years ago tree-ferns and tree-like clubmosses began adding oxygen into the carbon-dioxide atmosphere of this planet. This made it possible for life to evolve and develop into what it is today and, eventually, for the human species to appear. It is the first debt we owe trees.

But what is a tree? It has been defined as a perennial plant with a single woody stem which is capable of exceeding 5 metres in height. This is as good a definition as any, though honeysuckle or ivy

might qualify, so maybe we should add 'that can stand up on its own'. In this book this definition is not used strictly and many hedgerow species and shrubs are included that normally have several stems, seldom get above 5 metres and therefore may be described by purists as shrubs.

Tree fern

How a tree grows

Trees are quite unlike mammals, for example, or insects. There is the obvious fact that they cannot move – a fact that has had a big effect on their struggle to survive through periods of changing climate. There is the less obvious fact that in your body, or that of a beetle, the 'life', the vital organs, are inside, protected by bone or muscle, shell or armour. A tree is dead on the inside and only alive in a very thin skin just under the bark.

A tree has an inner scaffolding of dead wood that supports a series of small solar panels called **leaves** which collect energy from the sun and gasses from the atmosphere. These are mixed with water and minerals mined from the ground by the **root hairs** to produce growth and life, by the process of **photosynthesis.**

The mixing is carried on by the circulation of **sap** in a system quite like our own bloodstream. The 'live' part of the tree under the bark is a layer of cells called the **cambium** which encircles the trunk and every branch and twig. The sap rises up the tree in a layer just under the cambium and circulates back down in a layer just over it. These layers are renewed each year and the tree becomes a little fatter.

A tree does not have a heart to act as a pump to keep this whole system circulating. Yet a big specimen may have to move a thousand litres of water from ground level up 50 metres into the sky on a summer day. The physics behind this apparent miracle has only been understood recently, and there are still some mysteries. It has to do with the odd properties of liquids in very narrow tubes, the suction power exerted by water vapour evaporating off the leaf surfaces, and a rather mysterious pushing power from the roots that forces the first sap up the trunk of a tree in spring.

Under the ground
We still do not know everything about trees, and the least understood part of them is their roots. A tree has a lot more root than most people realise. Typically there is more wood below ground than above – it is not in such thick sections, but it often covers a much

greater area. One obvious function of roots is to anchor the tree so it does not fall down every time the wind blows or a few tons of rain or snow lodge on the leaves. But the chemicals the roots mine from the soil are vital to the health and growth of the tree. They are, in effect, its food. The processes by which 'feeding' takes place are complex and only partially understood. It is important to realise that trees, like all plants, do not actually 'eat', they drink – in other words they can only absorb nutrients in a solution of water. Bacteria and, in particular, fungi play an important role in this. The full importance of the

relationship between trees and fungi, in their roots and above ground, is only beginning to be realised. In many cases it amounts to total dependence, neither the tree nor the fungus could live without the other.

Bracket fungus on Birch

Types of tree

We all divide trees up into different types in our minds in a more or less scientific way. We think of evergreens and deciduous trees, of **conifers** which have needles and **broad-leaves** which have ordinary leaves, of wild trees and garden trees. Most of these are good botanical distinctions as well, though there are some awkward exceptions. The two main botanical distinctions are between gymnosperms (conifers) and angiosperms (broad-leaves). The angiosperms are further divided into dicotyledons and monocotyledons, but the only monocotyledons of any importance that become true trees are the palms. The botanists make these distinctions using small, often microscopic differences in the way the seed has evolved. Incidentally, **evergreens** do lose their leaves, but they do it in a much more regular way, throughout the year, rather than in one go in the autumn like **deciduous** trees.

Some of the 'false friends' to beware of are conifers that surprise by dropping all their needles in winter – larches are the commonest example, though there are others. Other 'conifers' have leaves not needles – the Ginkgo is a gymnosperm with true leaves. There are broad-leaved trees which have 'cones' – the Alder is a broad-leaved deciduous tree which has evolved a small 'cone' which floats on water to spread its seed along river banks. There are also 'broad-leaved' trees which actually have cypress-like scale leaves – the French Tamarisk falls into this category.

Evolution

To think about the evolution of trees we have to think about the evolution of forests, and we have to think in very large chunks of geological time – trees go back far further than we do. The Carboniferous forest of 400 million years ago which produced our oxygen-rich atmosphere persisted for an almost unimaginably long time in a world that was uniformly hot. The Tertiary period, in the much more recent past, perhaps between 40 million and 12 million years ago, produced trees as we know them today. What *was* different was the forest – it was boundless, stretching from pole to pole, and it had the same mix of species throughout.

The ice ages

At the end of the Tertiary came the Pleiocene and a slow cooling. Differences appeared between the mix of species in the forest at the equator and that further north. Then, about a million years ago, an unexplained disaster struck the forest: the **ice age** (or, to be more accurate, the first of four ice ages). Between the ice ages were pleasant, temperate periods lasting up to 60 thousand years called **interglacials**. We are probably in one today.

All this was a disaster for trees because they are big, long-lived things which cannot move. There is some evidence to show that ice ages come on quite quickly and trees are certainly particularly badly equipped to cope with their onset.

North America was badly affected by ice, which advanced as far down as the southern United States, but trees fared better there than in Europe. This is because most of the mountain ranges in North America run north-south and present no barrier to a species fleeing, generation by generation, from the ice edge, then moving back up in the interglacial. All the same, many species became extinct and others only hung on in tiny populations, like the extraordinary band of survivor species on the Monterey Peninsula in California.

The situation was much worse in Europe. East-west mountain ranges like the Alps and the Pyrenees provided a cold, insurmountable barrier to the retreating trees. Areas where they might have found refuge, like the ice-free south of France, were already so densely covered with vigorous vegetation that the retreating species could not find space to take root. Warm Atlantic islands gave temporary refuge, but when the ice melted the sea level rose and they flooded. Above all, the Mediterranean Sea cut off the trees from retreat into Africa.

Things were not all bad. The ice age accelerated the processes of evolution enormously. All those tree species dashing up and down continents at what is, in biological terms, breakneck speed provided the opportunity to create new species by hybridisation (see p.23) and mutation. And, to a large extent, all this is still going on. Tree evolution has become a much more active process. All the same, the ice left

Europe in general, and Britain and Ireland in particular, with very few trees.

The trees return

Between the time the last ice retreated towards the poles, about 12,000 years ago, and the time when rising sea levels cut off Britain and Ireland from the waves of re-colonising trees, we acquired very few species. Even if you use the broadest definition of a tree, Britain has under 40 native species, and Ireland under 30. Many continental countries have over 80 species and the list would run to over a hundred in North America.

When the ice retreated from Europe it left a real mess behind. Piles of sand, gravel and boulders littered a wet desert. Plants, including trees, came in by various routes over the land-bridges to the Continent and colonised the mess. Birch and hazel were the pioneers about 10,000 years ago, then pine and alder, followed by elm, oak, lime and ash, in that order. We know quite a bit about this process, including the dates the trees arrived and how common they were, because their pollen has been preserved in layers of peat and mud and can be identified and dated by experts.

Our ancient forest

Forest again covered Britain and Ireland. There were trees everywhere except on the highest mountains and in a few isolated spots that had no true soil. A squirrel could have travelled in the treetops from one coast to another without ever having to touch the ground. The mixture of species did vary a bit, new species arrived and upset the ecological balance, the climate was still changing a little from time to time and there were a couple of mysterious crashes in the elm population which may have been caused by Dutch Elm disease, or something like it. But basically things stayed much the same until 5,000 years ago.

Farming begins

What happened then was the start of another disaster for trees. Neolithic man, and woman, arrived. The New Stone Age had begun. There had been humans in the forest before but they were hunters and gatherers who fitted into the ecology just like any other animal species. Neolithic people were farmers.

All over the world farming starts in the forest. Primitive people do not have the tools to break up the grass sod of the plains – anyway, Britain and Ireland did not have any usable land that was not forest. What a neolithic farmer did was to wander through the forest until he found a particularly large tree and then kill it by taking a stone tool and stripping off the bark and the living cambium in a ring all round the trunk. When the leaves fell off the tree, or failed to open in the spring, the farmer planted his crops in the resulting patch of light. The deep leaf mould of the ancient forest was soft and easy to till, but eventually its fertility became exhausted and another tree had to be killed to provide new ground.

Lost giants

There is a theory that this process, carried on for many generations, has had an evolutionary effect on trees. The idea is that early farmers selected large trees to kill, and smaller ones were left to reproduce – in other words our oaks, elms and ashes today are smaller than those of 5,000 years ago. There is some evidence to support this from wood preserved in peat bogs.

Whether this theory is true or not, there is no question that the impact of people on the forest for the last 5,000 years has been disastrous. As people have multiplied and their technology has improved, the destruction of forests has speeded up. This is particularly true in Britain and even more so in Ireland. We probably have fewer trees today than any country in the world which can grow them and had full forest cover in the recent past. Tree numbers have increased a bit in this century, but Britain and Ireland are still not in a proud position.

Conservation and preservation

It is strange that trees and woodland are not more fashionable as conservation causes. There is, of course, a lot of activity aimed at saving tropical rain forests, and this is very important. Temperate forests, including the little bits of 'wild wood' left in northern Europe, also need attention and protection, but somehow it seems to be the rare birds, or the wetlands or the meadow flowers that are foremost in the minds of conservationists.

The importance of woodlands

The value of good mixed woodland is many sided. Good woods form a very rich habitat for birds, animals, insects and other plants – particularly ferns and fungi. Modern woods are often richer in this respect than the ancient forest was. This is because the ancient forest was what is called climax forest – a high roof of tall trees stretching over the horizon with a dark and rather empty floor. Modern woods are small and often have roads, rides and clearings in them. They have more 'woodland edge' habitat, which is far richer than the dark interior of the climax forest.

An indication of the value of woods as habitats can be found by looking at a list of animal and bird species that have become extinct in Britain or Ireland in the last couple of thousand years. Most of them are woodland species, and habitat destruction has been the main cause of their disappearance. Britain lost its boars and wolves, Ireland its woodpeckers and its nuthatches.

Trees and climate

Trees, as we have seen, are very sensitive to even minor changes in climate. But trees do not merely react to climate, they also create it. On a global scale this is a subject which is being very intensively studied, but it is still mostly mysterious. On a small scale it is more obvious. Drive or walk along a country road on a frosty morning and you will notice that the only place the ground is unfrozen is under a tree. They raise the temperature, sometimes by several degrees. They can also make rain. This time pick a foggy day when it is not raining. Stand under a tree, preferably one with a lot of small leaves or needles. It will be 'raining' underneath the tree. The fog condenses on the leaves and drips down as 'rain'. When redwoods were felled in the coastal range of northern California, streams that used to flow all year began to dry up in summer. The redwoods were tall and covered in countless small scaly leaves; the mountains were foggy but there was little true rain. Fog drip fed the streams.

So trees should be preserved as climate producers and also because they take carbon from the air and lock it up in their wood, which helps reduce the effect of air pollution.

But trees and woods also deserve protection for a reason that exceeds their value as producers of climate, reducers of pollution or providers of food and shelter to other forms of wildlife. They should be protected because they are beautiful. Have you ever meet anyone who did not like trees?

It is too late to preserve ancient forest in northern Europe. There is none of it left. Claims are often made that such and such a patch of oak wood is a survivor of the great forest that once clothed our islands. It is not. The opinion of most experts is that the nearest surviving scrap is on the borders of Poland and Belorussia. There are a few coniferous groves in the Vosges mountains of eastern France that may qualify and bits of old French hunting parks that have a dubious claim. The nearest thing to it in Britain is some woods of widely spaced Scots Pines in the highlands of Scotland, but even they do not completely satisfy the experts. All our woods have been felled and regrown or extensively managed at some stage.

Tree management

There is more than one way to grow trees. There are also fashions in forestry. Up to the 1860s practically all British and Irish forestry crops were broad-leaves. The main timber trees were oaks and the principal trees used for 'smallwood' were hazels, ashes and willows. This was changed in March 1862 by a naval battle in the American Civil War in which iron warships were shown to be better than timber ones. Navies stopped buying oak and many tree growers went bankrupt. This left foresters with a bitterness towards broad-leaved trees which lingers on to this day.

Commercial forestry

Nowadays practically all commercial forestry in Britain and Ireland uses fast-growing conifers introduced from other parts of the world. The main species is Sitka Spruce, though Norway Spruce, Larch, Douglas Fir and Lodgepole Pine are also important. The plantations are normally of a single species. Because Britain and Ireland have such little forest cover, forestry practice here has concentrated on creating new plantations on 'green field' sites, though the 'green field' is more often a heather-covered hillside. Plantations are first thinned for pulpwood and then clear-felled for timber. In other European countries, like France, there is more concentration on the management of mixed woods and selective felling.

Broad-leaved trees are just beginning to come back into fashion with foresters. This change has a lot to do with grant incentives from the European Union. Many faster growing broad-leaved species have the potential to be just as commercially attractive as conifers.

Coppicing and pollarding
Some tree species, most of them broad-leaved, can grow new shoots from their stump when they are cut. If the cutting is done a few centimetres above the ground it is called **coppicing** and if it is done a couple of metres higher, above the reach of livestock and deer, it is called **pollarding**.

Coppicing and pollarding are very ancient

Pollard Willow

and widespread practices that have now almost died out in northern Europe. The product is usually a long, straight rod or pole of timber, which is used for firewood, small carpentry work, or a number of specialised jobs – for example willow coppice for basket making, hazel coppice for wattles. The rods are cut on a rotation system, usually varying from one year to fifteen years, so the whole process is sometimes called 'short rotation forestry' and has the obvious advantage that no replanting is necessary.

One of the odd things that coppicing or pollarding does to a tree is to prolong its life – perhaps indefinitely. Hazel is a short-lived tree. Its life expectancy is probably 150 years at the very most, but 900-year-old stumps of coppiced hazel have been found, still alive and well. All very old oaks have been pollarded at some stage in their history.

One common way of managing woodland in the past was 'coppice with standards'. Most of the trees in the wood were coppiced on a short rotation, but a few widely spaced ones (**standards**) were allowed to grow on for large timber, which they did very well as there was nothing of their height close by to compete with them. Selected seedlings or single shoots from a coppice stump made replacements for the standards as they were felled.

Although coppicing is a rare form of woodland management these days, it is only in the twentieth century that it has become less popular and it is an interesting exercise to try to identify old **coppice**

stumps or '**stools**' in woods that otherwise look quite natural. There are also some signs that coppicing may be about to have a revival. It is an environmentally elegant form of land use with considerable opportunities for energy crops, sometimes called '**biomass' production**. The coppice wood can either be chipped and burnt in furnaces to produce heat or electricity or it can be treated chemically to produce oils or alcohol. There are some other uses developed for willow coppice that include sewage treatment, slope stabilisation and motorway fencing.

Hedgerows

Another important form of tree management that is sometimes overlooked is the hedgerow. There are trimmed and managed hedgerows in which occasional trees are left to grow on as 'standards', and there are overgrown field boundaries in which the whole hedge reaches tree height. Both are rich in wildlife, but particularly the overgrown variety. Many of our forest species of plants and animals have only survived because of the hedgerow.

Apart from being 'ancient woodlands', hedgerows are important because they form safe corridors along which species can travel from one isolated population to another. They also, quite obviously, have the greatest amount of 'woodland edge' richness of any form of wood.

An old hedgerow – there are thousand-year-old examples still around – with a good species mix is a fine, easy place to study and enjoy trees. This is one of the reasons why this book includes some smaller hedge species, like Blackthorn and Spindle, which are left out of many books on trees. But hedges are also under threat. Thousands of kilometres of them are grubbed up all over Europe every year to make way for roads and buildings and to make bigger fields for modern mechanised farming. Also tractor-mounted trimmers have made the overgrown hedgerow something of a rarity. Britain, England in particular, has suffered quite badly from this, though it still has many fine examples. Ireland has fared slightly better. But hedgerows, like woods, in both countries need the awareness and the activity of conservationists.

Exotic trees

Although Britain and Ireland have such a poor range of native tree species and such a small amount of their land area covered by trees, they are compensated by another form of tree riches. They have, almost certainly, the best collections of foreign trees of any countries in the world. These collections are not just in botanic gardens, they are also in the grounds of large houses, in public parks, lining city streets and in suburban gardens. One English nursery garden offers in its catalogue nearly 8,000 different kinds of tree and shrub! The bulk of the trees described in this book are foreign species introduced by man, though some of them have **naturalised**, meaning they have escaped from gardens and collections and are leading a wild life.

Street trees

There are several reasons for this richness. One is that the climate of these small islands is remarkably varied – parts of the south-west are for practical purposes frost-free and support subtropical species, other parts have a range of arctic and alpine plants. Rainfall is fairly heavy and well spaced through the year. Soils offer variety and richness. All this suits trees.

Another less obvious fact is that trees of the temperate zone normally only grow for quite a short period in the spring or summer. Britain and Ireland lie towards the northern edge of this region, which means there is a lot of daylight during the growing season, making it much easier for leaves to do their job.

Then there is the fact that the number of native trees is small. There are, for example, only two native evergreen trees in Ireland with one extra in Britain –

the Yew, the Holly and the Scots Pine, respectively (not counting Juniper and Box, which are seldom trees). This shortage provides an enormous incentive to people to introduce foreign trees for profit or ornament.

But the main reason for the richness is concerned with history and politics. The wave of tree movement around the world reached its crest in the mid-nineteenth century. At that time Britain was acquiring the largest empire the world has ever seen, and Ireland was part of that empire. British colonial officials not only exercised dominion over palm and pine they (and, in one or two notable cases, their wives) brought the seeds of the palms and pines home in their pockets.

Tree introduction is remarkably well documented. It almost certainly goes back to Roman times, quite possibly even earlier. There are some excellent books on the subject. Many of the pioneer collectors were extraordinary people and their biographies are fascinating. But the whole topic is a subject in its own right and not central to this book, which is primarily about the identification of trees. All the same, some mention is made of the native origin of most of the species described.

Breeding trees

Introducing a species from abroad is not the only way to get a new tree. You can also breed them. You can do this by **hybridisation** – the process of crossing one

23

species with another, usually a quite closely related one. Hybridisation also occurs in nature, sometimes to the bewilderment of naturalists.

You can also select a new **variety**. This is usually done in a tree nursery. The nurseryman watches his stock carefully and selects one with a particular feature, often a freak characteristic, and breeds from that. This is how most of the yellow, copper and variegated leaf trees are bred. It also accounts for the bewildering variety of most species of fruit tree.

Reproduction

The sex life of trees is a bit complicated. Some species have males and females, some are **hermaphrodite**, meaning a single tree has both male and female parts, and others manage even more complex arrangements. The purpose is to produce seeds to reproduce the species. The advantage of a seed for this job is that it offers the possibility of **cross-pollination** – of one tree fertilising another of the same species – which leads to genetic diversity which, in evolutionary terms, is a handy thing to have. When the most successful trees in a forest are pollinating each other the species slowly improves and weaknesses are not perpetuated.

Trees can reproduce, or be reproduced, by other means than seeds. Limes and Black Poplars never, or almost never, reproduce by seed in Britain. The other means of reproduction include **root suckers**, **cuttings** (this method occasionally happens in nature too, particularly among willows and along rivers) and by

Bramley Apple tree

grafting a bit of one tree on to another, which only happens in gardens and nurseries.

Many of the fancy cultivated varieties can only be reproduced by cuttings or grafting. All Bramley Apple trees are descendants of one parent tree that was planted in a garden in the English village of Southwell nearly 200 years ago and which is still alive. All Irish Yew trees are descended from a female seedling collected on a hillside in Co. Fermanagh in 1740.

Tree age

The mother of all Bramleys is a very old tree now. The majority of tree species are not as long lived as most people think, with a few notable exceptions. Birch and hazel commonly die of old age after about the same lifetime as a human, say 70 or 80 years, though occasionally they reach 150 years. But coppice stumps of both species can get very old, and possibly can live for ever if the coppicing is well and regularly done. Beech seldom exceeds 250 years and Scots Pine seldom reaches 300. Oak almost never lives up to its reputation for long life – there are some old pollards in southern England that are probably about 800 years old, but one scientist who has devoted most of his life to counting tree rings in oaks, both living and dead, has not found any over 320 years old among tens of thousands of specimens.

The longest-lived species in Britain and Ireland are Limes, Yews and, possibly, Strawberry Trees. They are all species that are hard to put an age to with scientific precision, but there are probably Small-leaved Limes in north-west England that are between 1,000 and 1,500 years old. It is almost certain that there are Yews older than 2,000 years and just possible that there are 5,000-year-old specimens. Strawberry Trees approach immortality and there is even more guesswork with them, but specimens in Co. Kerry may be several thousand years old.

In Tasmania there are trees that reproduce by layering (a branch touches the ground, puts out roots and becomes a new trunk) that may have preserved a genetic identity for 30,000 years. There are also some small desert shrubs in different parts of the world that approach that age. But the oldest full tree, growing in a normal manner, that has been scientifically aged is a Bristle Cone Pine growing in the White Mountains along the California/Nevada border in the USA – it is 4,900 years old (nearly half the age of the current interglacial). The next mountain range to the west is the Sierra Nevada where Giant Redwoods live a mere 2-3,000 years.

It seems that stress promotes long life in trees – rather the opposite of what it is supposed to do in humans. The Bristle Cone Pines grow in an icy desert well above the 'treeline', over 3,000 metres up, where the only moisture is a little winter snow. A place full of stress for a plant. Both the Small Leaved Lime in England and the Strawberry Tree in Ireland are small, isolated populations living far to the north of the normal range of the tree; another source of stress. The oldest Yew in Britain is probably the Fortingall Yew in Scotland, which is also outside the normal range of the tree. The oldest oaks that have been measured are either pollards (and pollarding and coppicing provide another form of stress) or are very stunted specimens growing high in mountains or on acid bogs, often exposed to strong winds. The great parkland specimens are invariably younger than they look.

Finding the age of a tree

There are several ways to tell the age of a tree. The best way is to try to find a written record of when it was planted. There are more of these than you might think, particularly for churchyard trees, trees on village greens and those on large estates. Failing that you can count the **rings**. Each year the tree grows for a few weeks or months in the summer and then growth slows down in the winter. This produces a series of concentric rings in a cross-section of the trunk, each one representing a year – count them and you have the tree's age. It does not work in the tropics where trees grow more or less uniformly through the year, and it has the big disadvantage that you normally have to cut the tree down. You can, if you know how to do it, take a sample through the tree with a coring auger and count the rings in that; the tree normally survives.

An easier but less accurate method is to measure the tree. Surprisingly enough most tree species get fatter by about 2.5 cm per year. You measure their waistline 1.5 metres above the ground and do a simple sum. If the tree measures 2.5 metres round, there are 100 cm in a metre, so this is 250 cm. Divide this by 2.5 and you get 100 – this is the age of the tree in years.

Measuring trees is a bit of a science in itself. The most useful measurement is the approximate height. If you are guessing, remember that tall trees are always overestimated and small ones are underestimated. Also, thin trees appear taller than fat ones, and if a tree has a spreading crown it is usually impossible to see the actual top from the ground. Very tall trees, say over 50 metres, seem shorter when you look at them from below and you may underestimate the height. For more accuracy you can buy a rather expensive gadget called a hypsometer or use a number of improvised methods involving blades of grass, rulers, pieces of string, a precise knowledge of how long your pace is and rather more confidence with trigonometry than I can muster.

Dendrochronology

Once of the problems with counting tree rings is that very old trees are often hollow. The **heartwood** rots out because a hollow, supple tube is a much better sort of trunk to have in high winds than a solid rod. Unfortunately, with the heartwood goes the ring record.

Tree rings contain other data apart from the age of the tree. Each one is different, and each has information about what the growing season was like that particular year. People called **dendrochronologists** have matched the tree ring pattern in several species to known dates and, using microscopes, computers and preserved fragments of wood, have made a complete record stretching back up to 10,000 years. This is a very useful tool. One of the first things it was used for was to check the accuracy of radio carbon dating. It showed the archaeologists that many of the dates they were working with were wrong: some very wrong. Stonehenge, for example, is a thousand years older than was previously thought.

Dendrochronology has also contributed a great deal to the increasingly important study of climate change. It has thrown dramatic light on early volcanic eruptions, which may have deeply affected the course of our evolving civilisation, and threw so much dust into the atmosphere that oaks virtually stopped growing for 20 years. And it is obviously immensely useful to archaeologists to be able to send a fragment of wood to a laboratory in Belfast or Arizona and get back the precise calendar dates when that tree was growing – one such test came up with the surprising information that a Viking longship raised from the sea bed in Denmark was built of Irish timber.

How trees grow

There is one other important fact to remember about how a tree grows. Many people assume that branches rise with the growth of a tree and that a mark on the trunk 5 metres up may have been caused by damage at ground level many years before. This is not true. A child's swing hung from a branch does not slowly lift out of reach as the tree grows. All growth is from stationary buds on twigs and the leading shoot. The trunk becomes fatter, but does not rise.

Growing trees

This is not a book on gardening or forestry, but it is likely that many people with an interest in trees will want to try to grow a few. The problem is not usually obtaining trees, it is finding somewhere to put them. If you have some land available, even a smallish garden, then the next stage is to think carefully about your aims. Are you looking for a purely ornamental effect, do you want to encourage wildlife, do you want to simulate a bit of wild wood, or do you want tree crops like fruits and nuts? Possibly all of these things, so you will have to compromise in the next step, which is choosing the species of tree to plant.

This book should help you make that choice. It is also useful to look at the trees that are growing well in the neigh-bourhood, either wild or cultivated. They should do equally well for you. Try to give special consideration to native trees – they have many merits and are rather neglected by gardeners. Be careful about planting a lot of trees with fancy leaf colours – you may become tired of them.

There is a lot of choice when it comes to obtaining your stock. You can go to a nursery garden or you can collect trees in the wild. Probably the most interesting and satisfying way of obtaining common trees is to grow them from seeds or cuttings. It is also cheap. Woods produce masses of seedling trees, most of which are doomed to die from light starvation. Saving them by transplanting them to your field or garden is an attractive option, but you *must* have the permission of the owner of the trees.

One problem is that the seedling should be moved in winter when it is dormant, and at that time of year many tree seedlings are hard to identify as they have no leaves. If you spot something you want in the summer, tie a small piece of white plastic around the stem and come back a few months later to find it again.

The smaller the tree you buy or collect the better it will grow, all other things being equal. A small and inexpensive tree often outstrips an expensive nursery specimen that was three times its size when it was planted. Also, always select the tree with the best roots, not the best top growth.

Your next step is to decide exactly where to plant the tree. Its eventual size is an obvious factor here, and problems can arise from planting a tree in the wrong place. Do not let these problems discourage you from planting a tree, but do seek good advice first. If in doubt, plant – it takes maybe 15 years for a tree to develop to a size where it is a nuisance and maybe 15 minutes to cut it down.

When you plant, look after the roots. Make sure they are damp at all times, are protected from frost and have enough space and reasonable feeding. The top growth will then look after itself. Be cautious about using stakes: most do more harm than good. If they are really necessary, perhaps in a very exposed place with poor soil, use short ones and soft ties (old pieces of hosepipe bent into a figure-of-eight shape and nailed to the stake are excellent). Check the ties frequently to ensure they are not rubbing or squeezing the tree.

A plastic tree shelter is excellent for making a tree grow tall quickly, but do not take it off too soon or the spindly tree will fall over.

Once the tree is planted make sure it has plenty of water for the first year or two. If this involves watering, use a large quantity (fifty litres) two or three times a year rather than a watering-can full once a week. Keeping grass and weeds down for a metre all round a young tree makes a huge difference to how well it grows. Remove the sod and replace it with a **mulch**. The best mulches are natural ones – large quantities of dead leaves are the best of all. Next best would be something like bark chips, waste wood, straw or hay.

Mulch around a young tree

Prune reluctantly. If a tree is developing an unpleasing shape, obstructing a path or refusing to flower and fruit, take off branches using common sense and be as neat as possible. The main thing to avoid is unnecessary damage to the bark around where you cut. The only exception to this is deliberate damage done in summer to the bark of some trees to shock them into flowering or fruiting – a slightly dangerous practice.

Give yourself access to your trees so that you can enjoy them: make paths around or to them.

Tree watching

Trees are capable of giving so much enjoyment that it seems a little odd that tree watching is not as popular as birdwatching. The two activities do have something rather surprising in common – binoculars are useful in both. Tree watchers use them to identify leaf details, seeds and flowers in high treetops, and for looking at the occasional bird. A hand lens can be useful too because very small details like hairs on leaves are an important aid in identifying some species. The other useful thing is this book, which fits in a small pocket.

When it comes to tree watching, most people like to know what they are looking at, so identification is important. It seems rather daunting at first, but rapidly becomes easier. It is best to concentrate on one species at a time, learning its characteristic profile and colour, as well as the shape of the leaf and the pattern of the bark. When you can make an accurate identification at 200 metres from a car speeding down a motorway, it is time to move on to another species.

Although botanists use seeds and flowers to classify trees, the most important features for an amateur naturalist are the leaves. Yes, you may complain, but suppose it is a deciduous tree and it is winter? In fact leaves are nearly always present in the litter beneath a tree all year round, except in very tidily managed parks and gardens. I once went out on a summer day with a great tree expert to try to find a rarity in a large wood. I walked off with my head in the air, looking at leaves and bark. He set off with his head bent down, looking at the ground. He found the tree and I did not.

When you have the leaf it may suggest something to you. Perhaps it reminds you vaguely of Sycamore, only it is different? You will find from this book that the Sycamore is a member of the maple family and all the maples are grouped together, so start there. This works about ninety per cent of the time, though it may fail with some species. If you are only familiar with narrow-leaved willows a Goat Willow leaf does not shout 'willow!' at you, and a Holm Oak leaf looks more like Holly than an oak.

There are other features you can then include. Seeds and flowers are very useful, but they are seasonal in most species. The acorn of Holm Oak would immediately set you off in the right direction. So, probably, would the catkin of the Goat Willow.

Bark can be helpful, so can the general size and profile of the tree, whether or not it appears to be evergreen and the location it is growing in. In some species smell and texture are important. The more different pieces of information you have, the more accurate an identification you will make.

Sooner or later you will be totally baffled by a tree. It happens to everyone, even seasoned botanists. There are so many very rare exotic species, so many hybrids and intermediate forms of trees, and so many new cultivated varieties produced from nurseries every year. Don't let it worry you.

Classification

This will probably bring you to a stage where you ask: what is a species, anyway? Like many good questions, this does not have a very good answer. A **species** is usually defined in botany as a group of similar plants that grow together in nature, breed together and produce offspring like themselves. This is not altogether satisfactory because there are exceptions. If there weren't exceptions, there would not be any hybrids, for example. One expert wrote: 'it's a matter of individual judgement as to what constitutes a species and what a variety'.

The only strong thing you can say in favour of the concept of a species is that if we abandoned it we would be much worse off.

This brings us to the question of Latin names. Many nature lovers are put off by Latin names, which is a shame because they can be quite useful when they are not just being used to impress people. The idea is to have a standard name for each species that is different from every other species, irrespective of language or regional variations of language, and that indicates where the species lies in the botanical scheme of things.

This is helpful because in Scotland Sycamores are often called Planes and in Ireland Willows are called Sallies, so the common name may be unreliable. It also means that botanists from different countries can communicate without knowing each other's language. It also shows which species are closely related to the one you are interested in.

However, it can also be unhelpful. There are several Latin names for many species and botanists sometimes change their minds about the relationships between plants. The amateur naturalist is better off trying to learn both the common and Latin names of trees. Also remember that Latin and Greek are dead languages, so nobody knows how they were really pronounced. You may make strange attempts at saying *Chamaecyparis nootkatensis*, but you cannot be wrong.

POSTSCRIPT

Books are the accumulated memory store of the human race. Nobody can write one without borrowing from the rest. I have gone frequently to the store and returned with much knowledge and some wisdom. I am grateful to all the other writers for this, but it does not seem fitting to single out a small list for named acknowledgement.

HOW TO USE THIS BOOK

In this book, the **family** name is at the very top of each page. This shows the main section that each tree or group of trees belongs to. The commonest English name for each species is given in capital letters on the next line. This is followed by the Latin name, which is normally two words. The first word begins with a capital letter and is the **genus** or group to which the species belongs. The second word begins with a small letter and is the name of the **species** itself. In full botanical nomenclature this is followed by the name or initials of the botanist who was responsible for the Latin name, but this has been omitted in this book. If there is an **x** in front of a name it indicates a hybrid. A capital **X** indicates a hybrid between two species, each in a different genus – very rare, but it does happen a couple of times in the tree world.

A name in inverted commas, which may be in Latin or English, indicates a cultivated variety. The word **var.** indicates a naturally occurring **variety**. The word **syn.** indicates a second botanical name that is in common use: a **synonym**. Any other commonly occurring English names for the species are noted further down the page under the heading AKA, or 'Also Known As'. At the beginning of the description of the tree is a small silhouette drawing which shows the shape of a typical specimen.

Most of the book describes one species on each page. There is an extra page for some of the larger groups of trees which gives brief descriptions of some rarer members of the group which you might come across. An index at the back lists the English names of the species described.

Key words

Throughout the book technical botanical terms have been replaced by simple English words, or where they are unavoidable, have been explained. This is a small sacrifice in scientific accuracy for a great saving in comprehension. There is an amazing amount of totally unnecessary jargon in botany – 'hairy leaf stalk' is just as precise as 'pubescent petiole'.

However, there are a few key words and ideas that may be difficult for those new to the subject. Most of these have to do with the shape and make-up of leaves. There are **simple** leaves like those of hazel or beech. Sometimes these leaves have lumps or points on them which are called **lobes** as in oak or sycamore. There are also compound or **pinnate** leaves like ash and elder where a single stalk has a number of **leaflets** along it. There are also 30 or 40 technical words to describe the shape of leaves, which have been replaced with easier words (acuminate becomes pointed, obovate becomes pear-shaped, micronate becomes spined). Some trees have **needles**, like the pines, and other have **scale leaves** - for an example of scale leaves see the photo of Lawson Cypress on p. 46.

Photographs

The photographs on each page have been chosen to show the most important details of the tree from an identification point of view. This is rarely the whole tree, more usually something like a leaf or leafy shoot. Extra photographs in the 'Tree Details' section at the back of the book show some additional features such as cones, blossom, seeds and fruit. These are individually cross-referenced within the description of the main page entry for each species.

The text

The short piece of text on each page provides some general information about each tree. It includes information on features that are likely to be helpful in identification, in particular, features like smell and texture which cannot be shown in photographs.

It is followed by up to four quick reference sections:

AKA	lists other common English names for the species, where these exist.
Height	gives an idea of the height of the tree, which is the most useful dimension. This is the maximum that a good specimen could reach under ideal conditions in northern Europe – in other words you will find plenty of smaller trees of that species, but very few larger ones.
Range	indicates where the species is most likely to be found in Britain or Ireland and gives some idea of how common it is.
ID	deals with recognition, picking out and describing the key points which will help you to recognise the species.

GINKGO *Ginkgo biloba*

An extraordinary tree because all the related species are fossils. It comes from China where it is planted as a temple tree, and may be extinct in the wild. Introduced around 1730 into Europe, where it is popular in parks. There are some ornamental varieties.

AKA Maidenhair Tree.
Height Over 30 m, but usually smaller.
Range Parks and large gardens. Rare in Ireland and Scotland.
ID Deciduous, unmistakable, fan-shaped leaf, split down middle. Fruit a large, egg-shaped, green berry, ripening to yellow (p.233), though seldom flowers or fruits in Britain. Winter profile can be confused with pear tree.

YEW *Taxus baccata*

A native European evergreen tree, liking alkaline soil. Nowadays it is uncommon as an individual tree in woodlands and is very rare as a grove. It is very long lived, some trees being several thousand years old. Most parts of the tree are poisonous to humans and livestock.

Height Up to 25 m.

Range Commonest in churchyards, parks and gardens, sometimes as a hedge.

ID Squat profile, with flat, bright green needles. Female has red fleshy fruit. Trunk usually fluted; bark red and flaky.

OTHER YEWS

There are other species of yew from different parts of the world, but they are very rare in Europe. However, the plant breeders have developed a number of ornamental forms of the common Yew. There are varieties with yellow fruit and ones with golden or variegated foliage. The commonest variety is the **Irish Yew** (**right**), which grows as an upright column and is often planted in church-yards and cemeteries. All Irish Yews are female as they are all descended from a tree discovered on a hillside in Co. Fermanagh around 1740.

MONKEY PUZZLE *Araucaria araucana*

A strange South American evergreen grown in European parks and gardens for about two hundred years. The distinctive silhouette of mature specimens and the unusual spiky foliage make this one of the easiest trees to recognise.

AKA Chile Pine, Araucaria.

Height Up to 30 m, tallest in W Britain and Ireland.

Range Parks and gardens throughout Europe, sometimes naturalised.

ID Domed shape with tough spiny leaves and dark grey wrinkled bark. Large green and yellow spined fruit contains edible seeds.

INCENSE CEDAR *Calocedrus decurrens* syn. *Libocedrus decurrens*

An attractive evergreen tree native to California and Oregon, USA. Its appeal lies in its neat, upright profile, sometimes pencil slim, and the strong turpentine smell of the crushed foliage, which gives it its English name.

Height   Over 30 m.
Range   An ornamental in larger gardens and parks all over Europe, commonest in England.
ID   Scaly, reddish bark; leaves with overlapping scales, green at first, then red-brown. Small cone, pale yellow in late summer.

45

LAWSON CYPRESS *Chamaecyparis lawsoniana*

A fast-growing evergreen from California and Oregon, USA, now very popular in Europe. The many ornamental forms all have a characteristic smell of parsley when the foliage is crushed.

Height Up to 40 m.

Range Small gardens, often in towns and suburbs, parks and churchyards. Sometimes as forestry plantation or wind-breaks.

ID Flattened scaly leaves with strong scent. Conical outline with drooping tip, trunk often forked. Dark bark vertically fissured in older trees. Small round cone, green, ripening purple-brown, wrinkled and woody.

OTHER FALSE CYPRESSES

The only other false cypress species commonly grown in Europe is the **Nootka Cypress**, *Chamaecyparis nootkatensis* (**below**), which is sometimes used for hedging. It differs from Lawson Cypress (opposite) in that mature trees have a smooth, conical crown, the foliage has a totally different smell (oily and rather unpleasant), the male flower is yellow, and its slow-maturing cone is bluer, slightly larger and spinier.

There are many small cultivated varieties of Lawson Cypress and some of Nootka Cypress. They come in almost all shapes and sizes and a variety of colours. The smell of the foliage is one of the few constant ID points.

LEYLAND CYPRESS x *Cupressocyparis leylandii*

This is probably the most commonly planted garden evergreen and is a botanical oddity: a hybrid between parents of two different genera, the true cypresses and the false cypresses. Its popularity comes from being very hardy and very fast growing. Large, mature trees are quite uncommon, smaller trees and hedges are everywhere.

Height   Up to 30 m, but usually smaller.
Range   Everywhere in gardens.
ID   Dark red-brown bark with shallow vertical cracks. Scale-like leaf, colour varies with different varieties; small round cone also varies.

MONTEREY CYPRESS *Cupressus macrocarpa*

An evergreen with a very small natural range, having survived the last ice age only on a single headland in California, USA. Often planted on coasts, as it is resistant to salt winds and is hardy and fast growing. Now less popular than Leyland Cypress (opposite), of which it is one of the parents.

AKA Macrocarpa.
Height Up to 40 m, but usually smaller.
Range Wind-breaks and hedges on N Europe coasts; as forestry tree in S Europe.
ID Lemon-scented, scaly leaf. Wide, cedar-like profile, often wind-sculpted. Brown bark with shallow ridges, turns grey with age. Large, round, lumpy cone ripens red-brown.

ITALIAN CYPRESS *Cupressus sempervirens*

A native of the eastern Mediterranean, widely planted in formal gardens all over Europe because of its unmistakable pencil shape. In southern Europe it is used for reafforestation, but it is under threat from a fungus not unlike Dutch Elm disease. In Britain and Ireland it is curiously uncommon, despite being frost hardy.

AKA	Pencil Cypress (sometimes, incorrectly, Pencil Cedar, see p.54).
Height	20–30 m.
Range	Formal gardens and parks in Britain. In S Europe also lining roads, in replanting and wild.
ID	Pencil profile, some wild trees spreading more. Brown-grey bark with spirals of shallow, scaly ridges. Large cone, very like Monterey Cypress (p.49)

Smooth Arizona Cypress *Cupressus glabra*

An American species, increasingly planted in European gardens because of its attractive blue-grey foliage, which stands up well to trimming, and its interesting bark.

AKA	Smooth Cypress and (incorrectly) Arizonica.
Height	To 20 m, but normally smaller..
Range	Gardens, occasionally as a hedge.
ID	Purple-brown bark flaking off to reveal red or yellow patches. Blue-grey scale-leaf. Purple-brown cone, retained on tree for many years after ripening.

COMMON JUNIPER *Juniperus communis*

Native all over Europe, Juniper adapts to an amazing range of conditions. A slow-growing evergreen, very variable in shape, it grows as a spreading mat, a shrub and occasionally a small tree. The berries are used to flavour food and gin. Wild Juniper is uncommon in gardens, but there are many cultivated forms (see p.54).

Height Occasionally 6–10 m, usually much smaller.
Range Wild across Europe on all soils, including to 3,700 m in the Alps.
ID Sharply pointed needles. Small yellow flower, male and female on separate trees. Small, round berry ripens on tree over several years, from green through blue to black.

OTHER JUNIPERS

There are a number of other juniper species in Europe and elsewhere. Most of them are not trees or are very rare. The only exceptions are the Chinese Juniper, *Juniperus chinensis*, which can make a slightly untidy looking tree of up to 18 m and is planted in town parks, churchyards and some gardens in Britain, and the **Pencil Cedar**, *J. virginiana* (**below**), from North America, which is really a large juniper up to 30 m in height and is planted as an ornamental in Europe and occasionally for its timber, from which pencils are made. However, there are a number of varieties of juniper that have been bred for gardens. Most of these are quite small and are often planted in rockeries. The commonest tree-size one is Irish Juniper, which makes a very narrow pointed column up to 8 m.

WESTERN RED CEDAR *Thuja plicata*

This North American evergreen is not a true cedar, though it is the 'cedar' of the timber trade. Yellow or variegated forms are increasingly planted in gardens, particularly in Ireland.

AKA Thuja.

Height Specimen trees can reach 60 m.

Range Occasional forest crop, particularly in Scotland and Ireland. Common as hedge, wind-break and specimen tree in larger country gardens.

ID Low branches may layer, forming extra trunks. Aromatic scale-leaf, dark green above, paler below. Dark purplish-brown bark often fluted in old trees. Small, leathery, urn-shaped cone. Very inconspicuous flower.

OTHER THUJAS

There are a number of other thuja species, mostly from the Far East, but they are rare in Europe. The North American **White Cedar**, *Thuja occidentalis* (**below**), is also uncommon as a pure-bred, but there are numerous cultivated varieties that are popular in gardens. Many of these are dwarf trees, some grow as narrow cone shapes, and the sprays of scale-leaves often have streaks of white, yellow or orange. One other species, the Hiba, *Thujopsis dolabrata* is fairly common in large gardens in western Britain and Ireland. It comes from Japan, its main characteristic being the bark, which flakes off in strips of red and rich browns as if a cat has scratched it. It was originally classified as a *Thuja* by botanists, but then given a genus of its own, *Thujopsis*.

COAST REDWOOD *Sequoia sempervirens*

A primitive but magnificent evergreen from the coastal hills of northern California, USA. Often quoted as the tallest tree in the world, but that may be the Douglas Fir (p.65). It is fast growing, unusual in a tree with a thousand-year life expectancy, and coppices itself vigorously. Wellingtonia (p.58) is much stouter with different foliage and Dawn Redwood (p.59) is much paler and deciduous.

AKA Sequoia.
Height To 112 m in USA, 40 m in Britain, 50 m in Ireland.
Range Coasts of Britain and Ireland. As a specimen tree in parks, large gardens and some small gardens.
ID Spongy, red-brown bark. Narrow, twisted scale-leaves on stems; stiff, dark green needles on shoots. Small round cone ripens red-brown.

WELLINGTONIA *Sequoiadendron giganteum*

The biggest tree in the world in terms of the total mass of wood, this species can live for over three thousand years. Found wild in isolated groves in the Sierra Nevada mountains of California, USA, it is spreading since it was found that, to germinate, the seed needs burned soil. Difficult to mistake for any other evergreen.

AKA Giant Sequoia, Big Tree, Mammoth Tree, Sierra Redwood, California Redwood.
Height 85 m in California, 50 m in Britain.
Range Parks, gardens and roadsides.
ID Mature trees have massive trunks and very soft red bark (p.233), often pulled at by people and birds. Dull green scale-leaves, pressed against stem when young, bristly when older.

Dawn Redwood *Metasequoia glyptostroboides*

A deciduous tree thought to be extinct for some hundred million years until found in south-west China in the 1940s. Its elegance, rapid growth in good conditions and the extraordinary story of its discovery, have made it popular for planting in Europe.

AKA Water Fir, Metasequoia.

Height 30 m+.

Range Gardens and parks.

ID Unexpectedly deciduous, like Swamp Cypress (p.61) but with brighter red-brown or orange-brown bark and larger, paler, soft, flat needles set opposite each other, turning pink or red in autumn. Small green cone and flower seldom seen in Europe.

59

JAPANESE RED CEDAR *Cryptomeria japonica*

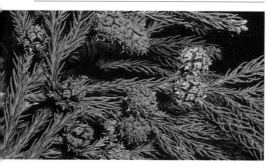

 This is not a true cedar, but it does grow wild in Japan and China with different forms in each country. In Britain and Ireland it is prized as an elegant park and garden tree that is hardy and fast-growing in western areas. The bark and profile are attractive and there are cultivated varieties, the commonest being 'Elegans' with slow-growing purplish foliage.

Height 30–40 m in Britain, taller in Japan.

Range Parks and gardens.

ID Red-brown bark peeling in strips. Cloud-shaped profile in a good specimen. Long, pointed, evergreen scale-leaf and small, round, spiny cone.

SWAMP CYPRESS *Taxodium distichum*

A very long-lived, deciduous conifer originating in swamps around the Gulf of Mexico. It produces aerial roots called pneumatophores, which help absorb oxygen and look like conical stumps sticking out of the water. Popularly planted near water in southern England for its unusualness or to reclaim wet land.

AKA Bald Cypress.

Height 30 m.

Range Beside or in water. Rare in Britain and Ireland outside S England.

ID Trunk often twisted with red, fibrous bark. Pale, spirally set needles on long shoots open blue-green very late in year, then turn green. Cone ripens purplish with a small central spine.

61

COMMON SILVER FIR *Abies alba*

Native to mountainous central and western Europe, but not to Britain or Ireland and not extensively planted today. It was once more fashionable; western areas have many old trees and it is sometimes naturalised.

Height Up to 50 m.

Range Mixed woodland and some old parkland specimens in Scotland, SW England and Ireland; occasional in rest of Britain.

ID Smooth, dark grey bark cracks into small square plates with age. Profile often deformed and partly dead. Needles dark green above with two white bands below. Large, erect, pointed cone on top branches only.

GIANT FIR *Abies grandis*

A native of the Pacific coast of North America where it has exceeded 100 m in height. In Britain and Ireland it grows faster than the Common Silver Fir (opposite), often replacing it as a pulpwood crop. Some regional native variations have been brought to Europe, causing identification problems.

AKA Grand Fir.

Height Up to 60 m in Europe.

Range Ornamental in large parks, rural gardens and estates; sometimes in plantations.

ID Needles with strong orange smell arranged like teeth of a comb, colour and size vary regionally. Cone smaller and smoother than Common Silver Fir.

NOBLE FIR *Abies procera syn. nobilis*

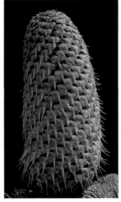

An elegant fir from western North America, becoming very popular in Britain and Ireland, mainly as a garden ornamental though it does not like urban conditions. It is the 'Nobilis' of the up-market Christmas tree trade.

AKA Nobilis.

Height 45 m, normally smaller.

Range Gardens and small plantations, particularly in W England, Scotland and Ireland.

ID Neat conical shape when young. Dense, stubbly blue-grey needles and massive, upright cone.

DOUGLAS FIR *Pseudotsuga menziesii*

 A very fast-growing conifer from western North America where it is probably the commonest tree. Widely planted in northern Europe, it is an important forestry crop in Britain and Ireland. It produces the tallest trees in Britain and holds the world height record (127 m) for a tree felled in Canada. The record for the tallest living tree is disputed between the Douglas Fir and the Coast Redwood (see p.57).

Height Over 60 m in Britain.
Range Plantations, wind-breaks and large rural gardens.
ID Dark bark deeply fissured when old. Medium-sized, shaggy cone hangs from ends of branches. Variably coloured, fruity-smelling needles grow from shoot in all directions.

OTHER FIRS

The Douglas Fir genus, *Pseudotsuga*, has only 4 other species, all extremely rare in northern Europe, but the Silver Fir genus, *Abies*, has around 50 species. Many of these are unlikely to be found outside botanic gardens or large private collections, but a few of them are less uncommon. They include:

Caucasian Fir, *A. nordmanniana*, from Turkey and the west Caucasus, a graceful and hardy tree with branches growing all the way down to the base of the trunk, even in older specimens.

Colorado White Fir, *A. concolor*, from the Rocky Mountains, USA, sometimes grown in gardens for its dense, blue-grey needles. There is a cultivated variety 'Violacea' with even bluer needles and a wild variety 'Lowiana', which is intermediate between Colorado

OTHER FIRS Continued

White Fir and Giant Fir (p.63), causing identity crises even for botanists.

Grecian Fir, *A. cephalonica*, from the mountains of Greece, recognised by the needles, which radiate all round the stem. It is locally common in parts of eastern England.

Delavay's Silver Fir, *A. delavayi*, from south-west China, has needles that crowd forward round the shoot and is quite frequent in Ireland, Scotland and western England. There are a large number of named varieties.

Spanish or Hedgehog Fir, *A. pinsapo* (**below**), an odd fir with a very limited native range in southern Spain. It has dark bark, very short needles and short cones, and mature trees have a dense mass of dead twigs protruding like spines from the crown.

Spanish Fir foliage

CEDAR OF LEBANON *Cedrus libani*

This Middle Eastern tree is very popular in parks and large gardens in Britain and Ireland because of its handsome spreading shape and the dramatic colour contrast of foliage and bark. The subspecies *brevifolia* from the Paphos mountains of Cyprus has shorter needles.

Height 40 m.

Range Parks, large gardens and churchyards, often in towns.

ID Distinctive profile, often broader than it is tall; trunk branched, foliage carried in massive flat plates. Dull brown bark networked with small cracks. Short, stiff, dull green needles. Compact egg-shaped cone (p.234). See also opposite for cedar identification.

ATLAS CEDAR *Cedrus atlantica*

A North African species with two forms: the green original form and a blue-needled variety (above) called 'Glauca'. The green one is hard to distinguish from the Cedar of Lebanon (opposite) and the Deodar (p.70), but if the tips of the young branches point up it is an Atlas Cedar, if they are level it is Cedar of Lebanon and if they point down it is a Deodar (Atlas Ascends, Lebanon is Level and Deodar points Down).

AKA Algerian Cedar, Atlantic Cedar.
Height 30 m.
Range Green form parks; blue form gardens.
ID Dark bark, often cracking into plates. Sharp, shiny, deep green needles. Cone smaller than Cedar of Lebanon.

DEODAR *Cedrus deodara*

A Himalayan species that is commoner in Britain and Ireland than is realised and is frequently misidentified (see p.69 for cedar ID). It is not a long-lived tree – up to a hundred or a hundred and fifty years – although it can become very massive.

AKA	Himalayan Cedar.
Height	35 m.
Range	Common in large and small gardens, churchyards and town parks.
ID	Dark bark often with a few black cracks. Needles variable, but longer than other cedars. Large barrel-shaped cone often hidden on high branches.

JAPANESE LARCH *Larix kaempferi*

This Japanese import is very popular in Europe, being even faster growing than the local larch. Its reddish bark is considered more ornamental than the yellowish bark of European Larch (p.72). The hybrid of the two species has many of their best qualities, but its timber is slightly inferior.

Height 35 m.
Range Increasingly in gardens. Some forestry plantations in W hills; wind-breaks, avenues and for land reclamation.
ID Reddish bark; dark orange shoot; grey-green needles. Cone dumpier than European Larch, scales turn out and down when ripe. Hybrids are hard to identify.

EUROPEAN LARCH *Larix decidua*

Larches drop their needles in winter; the only other conifers to do this are Swamp Cypress (p.61) and Dawn Redwood (p.59). European Larch is native to the Alps and other European mountains. Common and important in Britain and Ireland, it is planted as a forestry crop and an ornamental, because it is tough, fast growing, has an elegant shape and delicate foliage, and better quality timber than most conifers.

Height Up to 40 m in plantations, 30 m in the wild.

Range Gardens, plantations and avenues everywhere, sometimes naturalised in woods.

ID Yellowish-green bark; soft, pale green needles; flower usually mauve-red. Small compact cone often kept for years. Hybrids with Japanese Larch (p.71) are hard to identify.

NORWAY SPRUCE *Picea abies*

A European tree with a huge native range that has excluded Britain and Ireland since the last ice age. It has been widely introduced as a forestry crop, grows in many gardens and is the traditional Christmas tree. It is easily confused with Sitka Spruce (opposite).

AKA Norway Fir (incorrectly).

Height 40 m.

Range Wild across continental Europe. Plantations, gardens and Christmas tree nurseries in Britain.

ID Rough, thin bark, usually reddish. Long, cylindrical, cone. Needles shorter and greener than Sitka Spruce, pointing down the shoot. When shoot stroked downwards, Sitka pricks, Norway does not.

SITKA SPRUCE *Picea sitchensis*

Native to America's Pacific northwest, now the commonest tree in Britain and Ireland because it is the choice forestry crop on wet or acid land and upland. It is very fast growing and mature trees are considerably taller than any other spruce species. It is easily confused with Norway Spruce (opposite).

Height To 50 m.

Range Plantations in Scotland, Ireland, Wales and W England. Some old trees on estates, seldom in gardens. Sometimes naturalised.

ID Plated, purplish bark. Sausage-shaped cone, smaller than Norway Spruce. Short, sharp, blue-green needles that prick when shoot is stroked downwards.

OTHER SPRUCES

There are nearly 50 other spruces worldwide. In Britain and Ireland most are only found in botanic gardens and specialist collections. The most common are:

Oriental Spruce, *Picea orientalis*, a quite common garden ornamental in the cultivated variety 'Aurea' with golden-yellow shoots.

Colorado Spruce, *P. pungens* (**below**), a wetland forestry crop on the Continent, mostly grown in Britain as the garden ornamental variety 'Glauca', also called Blue Spruce because of its striking needles.

Serbian Spruce, *P. omorika*, sometimes used in forestry on alkaline land, but quite common as a garden ornamental with its attractive, slender profile and considerable tolerance of air pollution.

Brewer Spruce, *P. brewerana*, increasingly planted in parks and small gardens as it is slow growing and has unusual blackish foliage producing elegant curtains of hanging branchlets.

WESTERN HEMLOCK *Tsuga heterophylla*

Hemlocks are distinctive evergreen conifers with strong-smelling yew-like foliage and odd male and female cones. The Western Hemlock, from high rainfall areas of western North America, is sometimes used in European forestry, usually planted under broad-leaved trees as it is very shade tolerant. Also commonly planted for its graceful outline.

AKA	Tsuga.
Height	45 m in Britain, 60 m in N America.
Range	Occasional forest crop, also parks and large gardens.
ID	Elegant conical shape, slightly upswept branches, top shoot droops. Untidy needles. Bright red-purple male flower turns white in spring; egg-shaped female cone ripens green-brown.

EASTERN HEMLOCK *Tsuga canadensis*

This tree from eastern North America is less common in Europe than the Western Hemlock (p.77), but is the only other hemlock species likely to be found outside collections. It has no forestry uses, but is planted as an ornamental in drier parts of eastern Britain.

AKA	Canadian Hemlock.
Height	30 m.
Range	Parks and gardens, commoner in E Britain.
ID	Untidy profile, coarsely cracked bark. Smaller cone and needles than Western Hemlock. Needles in two neat rows along shoot.

Scots Pine *Pinus sylvestris*

A tree with a huge native European range including Siberia and the highlands of Scotland. Once extinct in England, Wales and Ireland, it has been re-introduced and is widely naturalised. Widely planted for timber, shelter and ornament.

Height To 35 m.

Range Wild in open forests in Scottish highlands. Naturalised on heaths and bogs elsewhere in Britain and Ireland.

ID Open, flat-topped profile in mature tree, some varieties without flat top. Flat blue-green needles in pairs; orange 'crocodile-skin' bark. Pointed, medium-sized green cone ripens to brown.

STONE PINE *Pinus pinea*

A native of the eastern Mediterranean, widely planted as a specimen and in groves on Mediterranean coasts for shade and its edible pine nut. A very distinctive tree, but compare with Maritime Pine (opposite).

Height 25 m.

Range Occasional specimen in parks and gardens in warm coastal towns in Britain, Ireland and elsewhere in N Europe.

ID Umbrella-like profile; paired needles; large barrel-shaped, shiny cone ripens from green to brown. Bark orange-brown with some vertical cracks.

MARITIME PINE *Pinus pinaster*

This Mediterranean coastal species is an important source of resin and traditional railway sleepers in its native range, but is more commonly planted in Britain and Ireland to control coastal erosion.

Height 30 m, often smaller.

Range Wild and planted on W Mediterranean coasts. In Britain and Ireland in sand dunes or as coastal ornamental, commonest in S England.

ID Taller than Stone Pine (opposite) with more open crown. Long, stout, pale grey-green needles. Narrow, pointed cone; dark bark, cracking into small plates.

AUSTRIAN PINE *Pinus nigra var. nigra*

A fine pine, native to the mountains of central Europe, planted in Britain and Ireland on alkaline soils for ornament and shelter. This tree and Corsican Pine (opposite) are regarded by some botanists as subspecies of the same tree and by others as separate species.

AKA	Black Pine.
Height	30 m+.
Range	In Britain and Ireland on chalk and limestone, often along railways or motorways.
ID	Tall with a dense crown. Very dark, almost black paired needles; shiny yellow-brown shoot. Scaly, coarse-ridged bark, colour varies. Pointed cone ripens from green to brown.

CORSICAN PINE *Pinus nigra var. maritima* syn. *P.n. laricio*

Botanists argue about the classification of this tree (see Austrian Pine, opposite), which explains the unusually complicated Latin name. It is native to Corsican and south Italian mountains and is an important forestry crop in parts of England on difficult soils.

Height 40 m.

Range Plantations in S and E England. Ornamental all over Britain and Ireland.

ID Flexible, twisted needle pairs, longer and paler than Austrian Pine and blunter buds. Bark usually loose and flaky, colour varies. Pointed cone ripens from green to brown.

BRISTLE CONE PINE *Pinus aristata*

This extraordinary tree has specimens that are almost 5,000 years old, the oldest authenticated living things. It grows wild at over 3,000 m on the California/Nevada border in the USA. It has only been in cultivation in Britain and Ireland for about 25 years, so only young trees are present. Botanists argue about its precise classification.

AKA	Rocky Mountain Bristle Cone Pine (incorrectly).
Height	15 m in America, 5 m+ in Europe.
Range	Gardens and collections in Britain and Ireland.
ID	Bright orange shoot with needles like a fox's tail. Old bark purple-red, trunk twisted. First year cone smooth and purple, bristles appear in second year.

AROLLA PINE *Pinus cembra*

A native tree of the Carpathians and the Alps,
where it is somewhat endangered. Uncommon in
Britain and Ireland, it is planted in large gardens
and parks and is the commonest of the pines that bear
their needles in bunches of five. It is normally seen in
Scotland as a smallish tree (under 20 m).

AKA	Swiss Stone Pine.
Height	25 m in wild, less in Britain.
Range	Parks and large gardens, particularly in Scotland.
ID	Dense, narrow crown. Short, dumpy cone. Hairy shoot; needles in bunches of five.

MONTEREY PINE *Pinus radiata*

A pine with a very small native range, surviving the last ice age on a headland in California, USA. It is widely planted in coastal areas of Scotland, western England and particularly Ireland for ornament and as shelter. The cone does not fall from the tree, so they are always available.

Height 30 m, normally less.
Range W Britain and all over Ireland, often near coasts.
ID Needles in bunches of three. Large, squat cone with a unique swelling on one side of base, held on tree. Dark bark cracks vertically.

LODGEPOLE PINE *Pinus contorta*

A western North American species (some botanists recognise several subspecies), widely planted as a forest crop on boggy land in Ireland and upland peatbogs in Scotland and Wales. It is now unpopular for planting, but many older plantations still exist and it has naturalised in Irish bogs.

AKA Shore Pine, Beach Pine.
Height 30 m.
Range Plantations on acid soil in Scotland, Wales and Ireland; sometimes in exposed upland gardens.
ID Short, green needle pairs in dense tufts. Very prickly cone. Rich brown bark breaks into squares.

OTHER PINES

There are over 80 species of pine scattered round the world. Some of those found in Britain and Ireland include:

Mountain Pine, *Pinus mugo* syn. *uncinata*, a small double-needle tree from the high Alps, sometimes planted in gardens – *uncinata* is the tree form and *mugo* is the bush form.

Western Yellow Pine or Ponderosa Pine, *P. ponderosa*, a large three-needled pine from western North America, quite common in northern Europe as an ornamental and occasionally in forestry.

Weymouth Pine, *P. strobus*, a tall five-needled pine with very long needles from eastern North America, introduced to southern England to provide masts for sailing ships. Some specimens still survive.

Blue Pine or **Bhutan Pine**, *P. wallichiana* (**opposite**), a five-needle pine from the Himalayas, fairly common in parks and large gardens and occasionally a forestry crop.

Japanese White Pine, *P. parviflora*, a five-needle pine that is most commonly found as a dwarf form in Japanese gardens.

Jeffrey Pine, *P. jeffreyi*, a tall three-needle pine from North America, occasionally planted in parks and large gardens.

WHITE POPLAR *Populus alba*

Poplars are quite confusing, with a number of hybrids, intermediate forms and cultivated varieties. The White Poplar (the leaves are white underneath) is native to a huge area of Europe, North Africa and western and central Asia, but is introduced into Britain and Ireland.

Height 20 m.
Range Planted or naturalised in Britain and Ireland along roads, garden boundaries, and in parks and sand dunes.
ID Medium-sized, untidy tree with two leaf forms: small and oval with wavy margins, or larger with (usually) five lobes. Male catkin red-purple; female catkin greenish (p.234). Ridged grey-brown bark.

GREY POPLAR *Populus canescens*

This species is probably a natural hybrid between White Poplar (opposite) and Aspen (p.92), and it is easily confused with both parents.

Height 35 m.

Range Locally common, growing as wild, often in river valleys, especially in central England and central Ireland.

ID Larger, better-shaped tree than White Poplar. Leaf grey and furry below, with slight lobing. Bark grey to cream with black pits. Male catkin ripens to purple-red; rare female catkin green, developing white wool.

ASPEN *Populus tremula*

A native poplar with a very wide range from the Arctic to the southern shores of the Mediterranean and right across Asia. It is very versatile, growing in a wide range of sites. It suckers freely but, over much of its range, does not reproduce easily from seed. The leaf is held on a long elastic stem that shimmers in the slightest breeze.

Height 25 m.

Range Commonest on hillsides in Scotland, but may be in almost any damp site in Britain and Ireland.

ID Shield-shaped leaf with irregular teeth, turns bright yellow in autumn and is slow to rot. Bark green-grey with horizontal strips. Thick, brown male catkin (p.235) green female catkin, develops white wool.

BLACK POPLAR *Populus nigra*

 A rather rare native of northern Europe, probably also native to southern England and central Ireland. Its natural habitat is on river banks as its seed needs exposed mud to germinate. Planted along roads, in parks and around playing-fields, factories and railways in the industrial Midlands of England. There are many hybrids, see p.96.

Height 35 m.
Range Wild on river banks, planted on industrial sites.
ID Massive tree, short, heavy trunk with large bosses, and large spreading branches. Dark bark deeply ridged. Leaf unfolds khaki, becomes bright green and shiny on a stiff stalk. Large, bright red male catkin (p.235); rare female catkin longer and greenish white.

LOMBARDY POPLAR *Populus nigra var. italica*

The well-known and unmistakable Lombardy Poplar is a variety of Black Poplar (p.93) and is always male. It is often planted in straight lines along roads and river banks in Britain and continental Europe, but the trees are then susceptible to wind damage and gaps occur.

Height 30 m. (Trees of this shape appear taller than they are).

Range Along roadsides, river banks and in parks, commonest in central and S England, uncommon in Ireland and Scotland.

ID Slim, upright form, no bosses on trunk. Bark smooth when young, then dull with shallow ridges. Catkin (male only) red, later dusted with yellow pollen.

WESTERN BALSAM POPLAR *Populus trichocarpa*

This poplar from western North America is named for its very aromatic foliage. It is the fastest growing tree in Britain, often at 2 m a year (in Ireland some eucalyptus species are even faster). It is sometimes grown for matchwood, and is common along motorways for shelter or screening. It may have a future as an energy crop for biomass production. See also hybrids, p.96.

Height 35 m.
Range Along roads, as a boundary, in gardens and plantations. May border softwood plantations.
ID Large, long pointed leaf on angled stem. Dull crimson male catkin appears before leaves; female catkin green. Grey-green bark, smooth at first, shallowly cracked when old.

Hybrid Black Poplars

These almost impossibly confusing hybrids are quite common. Most of them have the Black Poplar (p.93) from Europe as one parent and an American poplar, either Cottonwood, Western Balsam Poplar (p.95) or Eastern Balsam Poplar, as the other. Some of the commoner named varieties are:

Balm of Gilead, *Populus x gileadensis*, which is usually surrounded by suckers, with the Balsam Poplar smell, and a leaf that is pale green above, yellowish below, hairy on the veins and shaped like the ace-of-spades.

Black Italian Poplar or **Serotina**, *P. serotina* syn. *P. x canadensis* (**below**), a very common hybrid with many forms, having leaves opening red-brown, a goblet-shaped crown and a pale grey trunk regularly indented so that a disc cut across the trunk would look like a cog-wheel.

Variegated Poplar or Aurora, *P. x candicans* 'Aurora', the only one that is easy to recognise. It has startling pale green, cream and pink leaves and is often planted in housing estates and gardens.

GOAT WILLOW *Salix caprea*

Native to all of Britain and Ireland and most of Europe, it is rather variable, sometimes forming a tall tree with a single trunk, sometimes only a many-stemmed shrub. Carries familiar 'pussy willow' catkins.

AKA Pussy Willow, Sallow, Sally.

Height To 20 m, but very variable.

Range Woodland, scrub and road verges everywhere. Often colonises disturbed land.

ID Broader, rounder leaf than other willow trees, deep red hairy stalk. 'Pussy willow' male catkin, silver then gold, before leaves break (p.236); later female catkin silky green exploding with white cottony seeds. Smooth, pale grey bark, with wide brown cracks.

97

WHITE WILLOW *Salix alba*

An elegant, tall and slim tree which is native to Britain and capable of very fast growth. Old pollards are common as it used to be important for basketwork. There are many cultivated varieties (see pp.99, 100, 101, and 109).

AKA White Sally.
Height Occasionally to 25 m.
Range River valleys and damp places with good soil.
ID Narrow, pointed, silver-grey leaf, hairy below. Young twigs olive with hint of red. Dark grey bark, usually ridged or cracked. Male catkin yellow; slender female catkin green, turns white with seeds.

WEEPING WILLOW *Salix x chrysocoma*

 Several willow species and hybrids have been bred with a weeping form. The three main parents are White Willow (opposite), a rare Chinese tree called Babylon Willow and Osier (p.103). The commonest Weeping Willow is a cross between White Willow and Babylon Willow and is easily recognised. It is planted for ornament, often along rivers and around park ponds, but grows equally well in dry soils and is becoming popular in suburban front lawns.

Height 20 m.
Range Gardens, parks and river banks.
ID Drooping branches; narrow, pointed leaf. Pale bark, networked by small ridges. Male catkin yellow; female catkin almost unknown.

99

GOLDEN WILLOW *Salix alba* var. *vitellina*

A cultivated variety of White Willow (p.98), which it resembles in almost every way except that it has startling golden yellow shoots that are particularly ornamental in winter. All willows pollard and coppice very successfully. Golden Willow is normally grown in gardens as a coppice stump with a multitude of young shoots, though it can grow into a substantial tree if left alone.

AKA Golden Osier.
Height 15 m, often smaller.
Range Gardens and parks; occasionally to stabilise embankments.
ID Golden yellow shoots; otherwise as White Willow.

CRICKET BAT WILLOW _Salix alba_ var. _coerulea_

 A phenomenally fast-growing variety of White Willow (p.98) bred for the manufacture of cricket bats.

Height 25 m.

Range Field margins, ditches and small plantations in Essex and Suffolk, rare elsewhere.

ID Slender, purple shoots. Otherwise as White Willow, with bluer leaf, and more upright and cone-shaped profile.

GREY WILLOW Salix cinerea

 A species similar to Goat Willow (p.97) with the same distribution at home and abroad, though it prefers slightly wetter places and is much more commonly a bush than a tree. A subspecies *atrocinerea* is also found in Britain with rusty red hairs under the leaves.

Height 10 m, commonly less.
Range Damp woods and scrubland.
ID As Goat Willow, but narrower leaf and hairier twigs with ridges that are easiest to feel if the bark is stripped off.

OSIER *Salix viminalis*

Formerly the basis of the basketry industry, it was extensively cultivated in osier-beds or sally gardens on damp fields. Coppiced annually, it was never allowed to grow into a tree. When the industry declined many neglected osier-beds reverted to woods of small trees. Also found as an individual along river banks and ditches.

AKA Black Sally.
Height Occasionally to 12 m.
Range In neglected coppices, sometimes in active coppices. Specimens near water. Commonest in Somerset and S-central Ireland.
ID Pale, long, thin, slightly twisted leaf, white hairs below. Catkin hidden in leaves: small, stubby golden male; longer, green female.

ALMOND WILLOW *Salix triandra*

Like Osier (p.103), this was an important basket willow (and still is, to a small extent). It is probably a native of Britain and Ireland, but it has been a crop for so long it is hard to be sure. It grows most often as a tree in damp places with a history of basketry.

Height Occasionally to 12 m.

Range In neglected coppices, sometimes in active coppices. Specimens in wet, lowland areas.

ID Smooth bark, flakes off revealing orange. Hairless leaf long and narrow, though broader than Osier. Long, bright yellow male catkin; female green.

BAY WILLOW *Salix pentandra*

 Named Bay Willow because its leaves look (and, some say, smell) like culinary bay leaves, it is a native of the damper uplands of Scotland, Wales and northern England, but grows in lowland sites in Ireland. It is very rare in southern England.

Height 10 m, commonly smaller, often a bush.

Range Uplands of Scotland, Wales and N England, often by water. Bog edges in Ireland.

ID Rounded, dark green, shiny, aromatic leaf. Very long, striking, golden yellow male catkin; bottle-shaped green female catkin. Cracked grey bark.

CRACK WILLOW *Salix fragilis*

Called Crack Willow because twigs and branches crack off easily, it is native to England, Wales and south Scotland, and planted in Ireland and north Scotland. It has often been pollarded and forms hybrids with White Willow (p.98), which can cause confusion.

Height 15 m.
Range Normally beside water.
ID Regularly placed, long bright green leaves. Small, yellow male catkin; long, slender, green female catkin turns fluffy white. Scaly, dark grey bark, becoming ridged.

CONTORTED WILLOW *Salix matsudana var. tortuosa*

This is a gardener's curiosity and is increasingly planted. It is a variety of a rare Far Eastern willow with an unmistakable contorted profile.

Height To 15 m, but commonly smaller.

Range Gardens.

ID Short trunk, terminating in fantastically curled and contorted shoots. Distorted, boat-shaped leaf opens very pale yellow-green. Rather shiny bark, becomes grey and cracked with age.

SOME OTHER WILLOWS

The enormous willow family contains substantial trees, and plants that are only 3 cm tall when fully grown. They hybridise with each other naturally and very freely. Cultivated hybrids have been developed for basketwork, timber, ornament and many new applications, including biomass energy crops, sewage treatment, noise-abatement walls and slope stabilisation. This means that precise identification is almost impossible for the amateur. Two more species and two varieties that make full trees are:

Hoary Willow, *Salix eleagnos* (**below**), a central European species with very narrow leaves and skinny

SOME OTHER WILLOWS Continued

catkins, sometimes planted ornamentally in Britain and Ireland.

Violet Willow, *S. daphnoides*, which takes its name from the unusual colour of its bark. A south European and central Asian species, it is occasionally found in small gardens, parks and on motorway embankments.

Coral Bark Willow, *S. alba* 'Chermesina', a variety of White Willow (p.98), similar to Golden Willow (p.100) except it has bright orange-red shoots.

Silver Willow, *S. alba* 'Sericea' or 'Argentea', another ornamental variety of White Willow with striking silver leaves throughout the season.

Hoary Willow catkins and foliage

COMMON WALNUT *Juglans regia*

Walnuts have been cultivated since prehistoric times for their nuts and, later, for their excellent timber, which is used in fine furniture. Their exact native range is unknown, but is probably west Asian.

AKA English Walnut.

Height 20 m.

Range Orchards, parks and gardens, sometimes naturalised.

ID Leaf unfolds orange-brown, turns green with seven unserrated leaflets on a central stem. Cut twig shows chambered pith. Bark pale grey, becoming cracked. Fat, drooping, dark yellow male catkin; green female flower (p.236) inconspicuous. Wrinkled nut in smooth green fruit (p.237).

BLACK WALNUT *Juglans nigra*

An American species increasingly planted as it has most of the good qualities of the Common Walnut (opposite), but, in warmer parts of Britain and Ireland, is much faster growing. However, the nut is inedible. It is capable of making a bigger tree, but older specimens are still rare.

AKA American Walnut.
Height 30 m, normally smaller.
Range Gardens and orchards, often as young tree.
ID Usually at least 15 widely spaced and finely serrated leaflets on central stalk. Cut twig shows chambered pith. Dark, deeply ridged bark. Slim catkin.

DOWNY BIRCH *Betula pubescens*

Downy Birch is normally mistaken for Silver Birch (p.114) and there are intermediate forms, which are probably hybrids, that are difficult to distinguish. Downy Birch leaves are a different shape and are usually available in the leaf litter all year round. Downy Birch tends to prefer wet lowlands, Silver Birch drier uplands.

AKA	White Birch.
Height	25 m.
Range	Commonest in Scotland. Across Britain and Ireland on damp soils in groves and mixed woods. Rare in parks and gardens.
ID	Mature bark silver-white with horizontal grey or black bands and no diamonds. Branch tips do not droop. Rounded, single-toothed leaf. Slim, yellow-green male catkin; short, fat female catkin green turning brown.

SILVER BIRCH *Betula pendula*

A familiar, graceful tree, native to almost all Europe including Britain and Ireland. Can be confused with Downy Birch (p.112). 'Pendula' in the Latin name indicates that the ends of the branches hang down, but not all specimens do this.

Height Occasionally 30 m.

Range Wild in mixed woodland, or in small groves on mountains, heaths and bogs. Ornamental in gardens and parks.

ID Shiny red-brown bark when young, turning pinkish white with horizontal grey bands. Mature bark silver, fissured with black diamonds. Angular double-toothed leaf. Slim, yellow-green male catkin; short, fat female catkin, green turning brown.

COMMON ALDER *Alnus glutinosa*

 A fine tree, native to almost all Europe. It is unusual among trees because its root nodules can fix atmospheric nitrogen, making it an important pioneer species and soil improver of badly drained land. Its timber is useful, but it is seldom planted. Alder is the only broad-leaf to bear 'cones'.

Height	20 m (very occasionally 40 m).
Range	River banks, swampy places, as groves or mixed with willows, poplars, or Downy Birch (p.112).
ID	Young bark purple, turns grey, cracking into plates. Very round leaf, opens orange, turns dark shiny green. Dull purple male catkin ripens dark yellow. Female catkin ripens to hard green cone, becomes brown and woody.

GREY ALDER *Alnus incana*

A European native, introduced into Britain for reclaiming polluted industrial sites and, on a small scale in Scotland, as a plantation crop. It forms hybrids with Common Alder (p.115), causing identification problems. Other alders include an American species (Oregon or Red Alder, *Alnus rubra*) and a European species (Italian Alder, *A. cordata*) which are sometimes grown as ornamentals.

Height 20 m.
Range Collieries, spoil heaps, industrial sites and some small plantations.
ID Smooth, grey bark. Pointed, oval, strongly toothed leaf, grey below.

HORNBEAM *Carpinus betulus*

 Native to much of Europe, south-east England, and some isolated pockets in England and Wales. Can be confused with Beech (p.123), as young or trimmed trees retain dead leaves in winter, but it is a smaller tree. Ornamental varieties include an upright pyramid shape that is a common street tree in London.

Height 25 m.

Range Hedgerows, mixed woods and as groves in England, sometimes as old pollard. Rare in Ireland and N central Scotland.

ID Twisted, deeply fluted, grey trunk. Strongly toothed, dark green leaf with very prominent parallel veins. Short, green male and female catkin (p.237). Winged, three-lobed seed.

HOP HORNBEAM *Ostrya carpinifolia*

A south European tree, occasionally planted in Britain and Ireland. It resembles Hornbeam (p.117), but is not closely related. The timber of both trees was probably once used to make yokes for ox ploughs (horn-beams).

Height 15 m.
Range Gardens and parks, mostly S England.
ID Fissured, flaky bark. Hop-like clusters of pale yellow-green fruit in summer.

COMMON HAZEL *Corylus avellana*

Native to Britain and most of Europe, where it is the commonest broad-leaf on all except acid soils. Typically bushy and many stemmed, it occurs as an understorey tree or as groves; often a neglected pollard.

AKA	Nut Tree, Cob Nut.
Height	Occasionally to 12 m, very variable.
Range	All over Britain and Ireland in mixed woods, hedgerows and gardens.
ID	Shiny brown bark. Hairy, toothed, shield-shaped, deep green leaf. Brownish male catkin ripens pale yellow; small female flower, brown with bright red centre when ripe (p.238). White-green nut ripens pink-brown in green sheath, usually in small bunches.

119

OTHER HAZELS

Turkish Hazel (below), *Corylus colurna*, a species from the Middle East, is occasionally grown in parks and gardens in warmer parts of Britain and Ireland. It is much taller and straighter with rough, grey bark; for nut, see p.238. There are many varieties of Common Hazel (p.119) that have been cultivated for nuts or for ornament. The fruiting varieties have larger nuts, which are usually sold as 'cobs' or 'filberts', but are otherwise very similar. The three commonest ornamental varieties are: 'Pendula' or Weeping Hazel, 'Fusco-rubra' with purple leaves, and the increasingly popular 'Contorta' or Corkscrew Hazel – small with exotically twisting stems.

ROBLE BEECH *Nothofagus obliqua*

One of the Southern Beeches (p.122), a group of beech-like trees from the southern hemisphere that is being increasingly planted in Britain. Roble Beech is deciduous.

AKA Nothofagus.
Height 30 m.
Range Gardens, parks and plantations.
ID Long, oval, toothed leaf, slightly beech-like, with 7–11 pairs of impressed veins (see photo p.122). Smooth, pale grey bark, later darkens and cracks into squares. Inconspicuous flower ripens into small bright green fruit at base of each leaf. Slender profile with very regular herring-bone shoots that hang down.

OTHER SOUTHERN BEECHES

A group of about 20 beech-like species native to the southern part of South America, Australia, New Zealand and New Guinea. Some are evergreen and some deciduous. They are used as an experimental tree in hardwood forestry plantations and ornamentally, as most are remarkably fast growing and make handsome specimens. Apart from Roble Beech (p.121), the three commonest species in Europe are:

Rauli Beech, *Nothofagus procera*, a deciduous species growing to 30 m, found in parks and gardens and some small plantations. The distinctive leaf is 4–8 cm with 15–20 prominent, impressed pairs of veins (below; the smaller leaf is that of Roble Beech).

Antarctic Beech, *N. antarctica*, a deciduous species that is much smaller (to 15 m) and only found in gardens and some parks. The crinkled leaf has 4–5 pairs of veins.

Silver Beech, *N. menziesii*, a small evergreen species (to 15 m), mostly in gardens in Ireland and Cornwall, with a small leaf (1 cm x 1 cm) and distinctive cherry-like bark.

Top: Roble Beech leaf
Bottom: Rauli Beech leaf

BEECH *Fagus sylvatica*

 Native to most of Europe, but introduced into Britain and Ireland except for south-east England and some isolated pockets. A tall, broad, handsome tree, important for timber, and a component of the ancient forest of Europe. The leaves are retained through the winter on young trees and hedges. There are many ornamental varieties (see p.124).

Height	Occasionally to 40 m.
Range	Mixed woods, groves, wind-breaks and hedges. Specimen in parks and large gardens.
ID	Smooth, silver-grey bark often green with algae. Long, pointed brown buds. Oval, shiny green leaf with prominent veins, rich brown in autumn. Bristly nut or mast contains four, fluted, glossy brown kernels.

ORNAMENTAL BEECHES

The Common Beech (p.123) has been bred in a number of ornamental shapes and colours to adorn gardens and parks. Some of the commonest are:

'Purpurea' or **Copper Beech (below)**, with many colour forms that are very commonly planted as specimen trees or alternating with green beeches in hedges.

'Dawyck' or 'Fastigiata' or Dawyck Beech, which grows in an upright column like Lombardy Poplar (p.94) and often lines roads or avenues.

'Pendula' or Weeping Beech, which grows like Weeping Willow (p.99) and is usually found in parks.

'Asplenifolia' or 'Laciniata' or 'Heterophylla' or Cut-leaf Beech or Fern-leaf Beech, coming in a wide variety of forms with the leaves cut, lobed or willow-like and occasionally exotically coloured. It is found in parks and gardens, and is common in the city of Bath.

SWEET CHESTNUT *Castanea sativa*

A vigorous and long-lived tree, native to southern Europe, North Africa and the Near East. It was a very early introduction to Britain and a much later one to Ireland. The nuts are only edible in good summers in more favoured parts of Britain and Ireland. The leaf is one of the largest in Britain.

AKA Spanish Chestnut.

Height 30 m.

Range Plantations and coppice woods in S England; specimen in parks and gardens elsewhere. Sometimes naturalised.

ID Old bark has parallel ridges, usually spiralling. Very large, long, dark green leaf. Nut has spiny green shell with two brown kernels.

PEDUNCULATE OAK *Quercus robur*

 A massive tree that was the dominant species of the ancient broad-leaf forest of northern Europe on heavier and more acid soils, and is native to all Britain and Ireland. It is not as long-lived as people believe, trees over 350 years old are all pollards. The different oak species are difficult to distinguish.

AKA English Oak.
Height 40 m as specimen, 20 m as forest tree.
Range Mixed woods, groves, hedgerows, parkland, parks and gardens. Sometimes as an old pollard, in old plantations or as a standard or stool in coppice wood.
ID Pale grey bark, cracks vertically. Lobed leaf on short stalk; acorn on long stalk.

SESSILE OAK *Quercus petraea*

The only other oak species native to Britain and Ireland, along with Pedunculate Oak (opposite). Sessile Oak is identified by having a distinct stalk on its leaf, but none on the acorn; Pedunculate Oak is the exact opposite. Intermediate forms, which may be hybrids, also occur.

AKA Durmast Oak.

Height 40 m.

Range Often mixed with Pedunculate Oak, but dominant in N and W Britain and on poorer soils, in mixed woods, plantations, hedgerows, coppices, parkland, parks and gardens.

ID Taller, slimmer, less massive tree than Pedunculate Oak. Bark longer, straighter fissures with less cracks.

RED OAK *Quercus rubra*

 The commonest of the many American oaks in Britain and Ireland, where it is popular because of its fast growth rate and magnificent autumn colours. Though it is usually an ornamental, there has been some experimental forestry planting.

Height 25 m, occasionally to 35 m.
Range Parks and gardens, occasionally in small plantations.
ID Large, deeply lobed leaf is variable. Smooth, silvery bark.

OTHER AMERICAN OAKS

There are over 800 oak species worldwide, and most of them will grow in north-west Europe. The commonest of the New World oaks found in Britain and Ireland is the Red Oak (opposite), but other American species that may be seen include:

Scarlet Oak, *Quercus coccinea* (**below**), grown in parks, gardens and on road verges for its autumn colour like Red Oak, with which it is sometimes confused, though its leaf is smaller, slimmer and much more irregularly lobed.

Black or Quercitron Oak, *Q. velutina*, mostly confined to Ireland and milder parts of England. The characteristic bark has square plates showing orange in the cracks.

Pin Oak, *Q. palustris*, mostly confined to southern England, with very deeply lobed, feathery leaves.

Willow Oak, *Q. phellos*, found in large gardens in southern England and Ireland. The leaf is a unique, slim, unlobed shape, like White Willow (p.98).

TURKEY OAK *Quercus cerris*

 A south European oak that has naturalised in southern England, is widely planted in the rest of Britain, but is uncommon in Ireland. Mature acorns are found on two-year-old wood, not new growth.

Height 35 m.

Range Naturalised in woods and hedges in S England, planted in parks and on road verges in rest of Britain.

ID Dull, dark green leaf, usually hairy below, with deep, regular, nearly triangular lobes. Whiskers form around the bud and persist at the base of the leaf.

DOWNY OAK *Quercus pubescens*

A tree with a huge range in central and southern Europe and the Near East, where it grows on dry limestone slopes. In Britain it is normally a small tree or shrub growing in southern parks and gardens. It is very similar to Sessile Oak (p.127), but is hairier. It forms hybrids readily with Sessile Oak and other oak species, causing identification headaches.

AKA White Oak.
Height 20 m, often smaller.
Range Gardens and some parks in S England and Ireland.
ID Hairs on twigs, leaf stalks and underneath the leaves.

HOLM OAK *Quercus ilex*

A native tree of the Mediterranean and as far north as Brittany, this is the commonest evergreen oak found in Britain and Ireland and is quite distinctive. Well-grown British and Irish specimen trees are far larger than the wild tree, which is often little more than a shrub. It is long lived.

AKA Ilex, Evergreen Oak (both incorrect).
Height 25 m.
Range Parks, gardens and lining streets, commonest in W and coastal areas. Sometimes naturalised in S England.
ID Shiny leaf black-green above, fawn and hairy below, varies in size and shape. Acorn in deep cup.

OTHER EVERGREEN OAKS

There are several evergreen oaks, mostly small trees from the dry scrub of southern Europe. The Holm Oak (opposite) is by far the commonest in Britain and Ireland, but three others that may occasionally be encountered are:

Round-leaved Oak, *Quercus rotundifolia* (**below**), from south-west Europe, which is a smaller tree than Holm Oak with a much broader and rather grey leaf.

Holly Oak or Kermes Oak, *Q. coccifera*, from south-east Europe, which is another small tree with quite distinctive holly-like leaves.

Cork Oak, *Q. suber*, a native of Spain and Portugal, is widely planted in North Africa and Sardinia. It is sometimes found in parks and large gardens in south-west England and south-west Ireland. The dull grey bark has thick flanges of finely ridged cork. In southern countries the outer bark is harvested as cork, revealing the dramatic orange-red inner bark.

SPANISH OAK (Lucombe Oak) *Quercus x hispanica* ('Lucombeana')

The Spanish Oak is a natural hybrid between Turkey Oak (p.130) and Cork Oak (p.133) occurring in southern Europe. The Lucombe Oak is an English cultivated hybrid with the same two parents. It looks like a Cork Oak without the corky bark, but it is quite variable in form causing identification problems.

Height 30 m.

Range Common in parks and gardens in SW England, less common elsewhere in S England. Rare in rest of Britain and Ireland.

ID 'Half-evergreen' habit (drops leaves in spring). Leaf varies but normally has 3-7 lobes on each side tipped by a spine. Acorns very small.

WYCH ELM *Ulmus glabra*

 Native to most of Europe including Britain and Ireland, where it is the only commonly found elm. Formerly a component of ancient forest, it has been decimated by Dutch Elm disease and is commonest today as a dead tree surrounded by live root suckers. In all elms the base of the leaf extends further down the stalk on one side than the other, in Wych Elm the long side crosses over the short stalk and hides it. There are ornamental varieties with coloured foliage or a weeping habit.

Height 40 m, but live trees rare at this size.
Range Across Britain and Ireland in mixed woods, hedgerows, town parks and churchyards.
ID Very large, rough leaf, size and shape varies. Seed pale green membrane with nutlet in centre.

ENGLISH ELM *Ulmus procera*

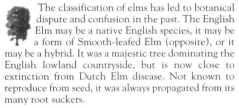

The classification of elms has led to botanical dispute and confusion in the past. The English Elm may be a native English species, it may be a form of Smooth-leafed Elm (opposite), or it may be a hybrid. It was a majestic tree dominating the English lowland countryside, but is now close to extinction from Dutch Elm disease. Not known to reproduce from seed, it was always propagated from its many root suckers.

Height   35 m, but live trees very rare at this size.
Range   England, less common in N, SE and SW, rare in Scotland and Ireland. Declining rapidly.
ID   Small, very round, dark green leaf.

SMOOTH-LEAFED ELM *Ulmus carpinifolia syn. minor syn. nitens*

A tree with a European distribution and many geographical variations. One is claimed to be native to south-east England, which is unlikely, and another to south-west Ireland, which is even less likely. They are probably an early introduction to both countries.

AKA	Small-leaved Elm, Cornish Elm, Wheatley Elm, Plot or Lock Elm.
Height	30 m, but live trees of this size very rare.
Range	Common in S and E England before Dutch Elm disease, elsewhere locally common.
ID	Small leaf, narrower than English Elm (opposite), unequal base joins stalk at right angles. Oval wings on seed.

DUTCH ELMS *Ulmus x hollandica*

 A group of hybrids between Wych Elm (p.135) and Smooth-leafed Elm (p.137) of which two were common in the south and Midlands of England before Dutch Elm disease. These were Dutch Elm, sometimes called *Ulmus major*, but more often *U. x hollandica*, and Huntingdon or Chichester Elm, sometimes called *U. vegeta*, but more often *U. x hollandica* 'Vegeta', which may be extinct.

Height 25 m, Huntingdon Elm taller.
Range Dutch Elm: S and Midlands of England, much reduced. Huntingdon Elm: S England, possibly extinct.
ID Longer stalk, smoother leaf than Wych Elm, with seed not in middle of fruit. Huntingdon Elm: taller, straighter more upright profile.

OTHER ELMS

There are about 150 elm species worldwide, originally poorly classified. This is being sorted out, but the trees are dying of Dutch Elm disease, which is basically incurable though some resistant hybrids have been bred. The most likely species in gardens and collections are:

European White Elm or **Fluttering Elm**, *Ulmus laevis* syn. *effusa* syn. *pedunculata* syn. *racemosa* (**below**), a central European native occasionally in cultivation in Britain and Ireland with very long stalked flowers.

Caucasian Elm, *Zelkova carpinifolia* syn. *crenata*, which is not a true elm, but a member of a small related genus. It is grown as an ornamental in parks and large gardens because it normally has a strange, oval profile with many stems erupting from a short, stout trunk.

Keaki, *Z. serrata* syn. *acuminata*, a Japanese *Zelkova* grown in parks and gardens, mainly for its pink, brown and orange bark with horizontal banding.

SOUTHERN NETTLE TREE *Celtis australis*

A common tree or large shrub in southern Europe, North Africa and the Near East, growing wild, planted as an ornamental or for reafforestation of difficult terrain. It is uncommon as an ornamental in Britain and Ireland because it is susceptible to late frosts. The tree bears hermaphrodite and male flowers at the same time.

Height   20 m, often smaller.
Range   Wild and planted in S Europe. Uncommon in gardens in milder parts of Britain and Ireland.
ID   Unusual leaf drawn out to a long twisted point with soft, pale hairs below. Smooth grey bark. Edible berry on long stalk, ripens through dull red to dull violet.

BLACK MULBERRY *Morus nigra*

 A native of south-west Asia that has long been grown in Europe for its fruit and as food for silkworms, though the White Mulberry (p.142) was the principal silkworm species.

AKA Common Mulberry.
Height 12 m.
Range Quite common in old orchards and parks, chiefly S England and Ireland.
ID When old, massive trunk leaning or even lying down on ground. Dark orange bark with many bosses and burrs. Large, oval, toothed leaf. Unmistakable fruit, like a loganberry.

WHITE MULBERRY *Morus alba*

 A Chinese species long cultivated in Europe as food for silkworms, though its pale fruit is also edible. It became rare in Britain and Ireland, but recently is increasingly planted in gardens and orchards. It is a more elegant and slender tree than the Black Mulberry (p.141).

Height 15 m.
Range Old orchards and gardens in England, S Scotland and Ireland, some more recent planting everywhere.
ID Pale fruit; smooth, hairless shoots. Smooth-topped leaf commonly lobed (occasionally so in the Black Mulberry).

PAPER MULBERRY *Broussonetia papyrifera*

This Chinese and Japanese species belongs to a separate genus from the true mulberries. It has been grown in Europe for some time as an ornamental and, in some southern countries, as a shade tree and street tree.

Height 15 m.
Range Occasional in British and Irish gardens and parks, commoner in S Europe as an ornamental and street tree.
ID Spreading profile. Odd female flowers are hairy green balls turning into orange fruit.

FIG *Ficus carica*

Figs are cultivated commercially in many parts of the world with a Mediterranean type of climate. In England and Ireland they are grown under glass, in basement gardens in large towns, in walled gardens and occasionally out in the open. There are several cultivated varieties, the commonest in Britain and Ireland is 'Brown Turkey'. The pear-shaped figs are normally present all year round at some stage of maturity.

Height 10 m, usually smaller.
Range Gardens in Britain and Ireland, commoner in S and W.
ID Smooth, silvery bark; large, lobed leaf.

EVERGREEN MAGNOLIA *Magnolia grandiflora*

There are about 80 species of magnolia native to America and Asia. Some are grown in gardens and parks in Britain and Ireland for their large, fragrant flowers, though most are not fully frost hardy. Evergreen Magnolia, the only evergreen, is the commonest species in England; Campbell's Magnolia, *M. campbellii*, is almost as common in Ireland. There are many hybrids and cultivated varieties.

AKA	Bull Bay.
Height	*M. grandiflora*: 10 m; *M. campbellii*: 20 m.
Range	Sheltered gardens in England and Ireland, *M. grandiflora* usually against a wall.
ID	Both species have grey bark and large shiny green leaves. *M. grandiflora* has white flowers, *M. cambellii* pink.

TULIP TREE *Liriodendron tulipifera*

A North American species, widely grown in England for its fine flowers and curious leaves, which give good autumn colour. It is rare in Scotland and Ireland and uncommon in Wales.

Height 30 m.

Range Gardens, parks and as occasional street tree in England, commonest in S. Rare in rest of Britain and Ireland.

ID Unmistakable leaf, reminiscent of a cat's face. Green and orange flower, more like a water lily than a tulip.

CHILEAN FIREBUSH *Embothrium coccineum*

A South American species, common in gardens in western and southern England, west Scotland and Ireland, but uncommon elsewhere. The flowers are unmistakable and the seed capsules are equally distinctive. The leaf varies and there are some cultivated varieties.

Height 12 m.
Range Gardens in W and S England, W Scotland and Ireland.
ID Slender and upright, with dark purple-brown bark. Flowers are spectacular bunches of scarlet tubes. Long, pointed dark red terminal buds; side buds oval and purple. Seeds borne in an oblong, grooved, buff-pink capsule with a dark red tip.

BAY TREE *Laurus nobilis*

This small tree, often only a shrub, is the source of bay leaves used in cooking and for wreaths to crown classical heroes. Originally a plant of the Mediterranean dry scrub, it has been much planted since ancient times. In Britain and Ireland it is commonly a tub tree or garden shrub, sometimes pruned as a standard, and occasionally a substantial tree. It is not totally frost hardy.

AKA Sweet Bay, Bay Laurel, Poet's Laurel.
Height 15 m, usually less.
Range Gardens in sheltered areas of Britain and Ireland, often in a container.
ID Narrow, finely toothed leaf with dark red veins at base; purple-red shoot.

SWEET GUM *Liquidambar styraciflua*

 This North American tree, quite common in southern England and southern Ireland, is rarer elsewhere despite being extremely hardy. On the Continent it is sometimes grown for its timber, and in the USA its resin has some commercial value. Ornamentally, its merit is in the autumn colour of the leaf, similar to the leaf of a maple, with they are commonly confused.

Height 20 m.
Range Parks and gardens, S and Midlands of England, S Ireland, sometimes elsewhere.
ID Alternate leaves, not opposite as in all maples. Resin and crushed leaf smell of sweet lemon soap. Curved dark purplish-brown pairs of fruit form a rough globe.

PERSIAN IRONWOOD *Parrotia persica*

 A common ornamental tree, grown for its flowers and its distinctive leaves with beautiful autumn colouring, as shown above.

Height 10 m, often smaller.

Range Large gardens, some parks and small gardens, commonest in S and W England.

ID Flower with bunches of deep red stamens (p.239), develops into shiny, brown nut in green sheath. Leaf opens bright gloss-green, darkens, then develops yellow, orange and crimson in September.

LONDON PLANE *Platanus x hispanica*

A hybrid tree of uncertain origin, remarkable because it is the best large tree to grow in cities – it tolerates air pollution, bad soils, trimming and pollarding and does not fall unexpectedly. It is long-lived and has the capacity to become the tallest broad-leaf tree in Europe.

Height 40 m, often trimmed or pollarded.
Range Urban streets, parks and squares, some large gardens. Less common in Scotland.
ID Distinctive, grey-brown bark, flakes to reveal large yellow patches, not so obvious in old trees. Five-lobed leaf resembles a maple, but varies between varieties. Flower a round ball on long stalk (above and p.239), ripens to prickly round fruit.

151

HIMALAYAN TREE COTONEASTER *Cotoneaster frigidus*

 Cotoneasters are very popular garden shrubs, but this species is the only one that makes a true tree. It sometimes hybridises with smaller species.

Height 15 m.

Range Larger gardens and some parks, particularly in W Britain and Ireland.

ID Sprouty trunk often leaning at an angle; pale bark. Semi-evergreen leaf. Small, round, hard berry, in clusters, ripening red.

HAWTHORN *Crataegus monogyna*

A very common and widely distributed small European tree. It is often a shrub, in hedgerows or scrub, and occurs as a true tree, in mixed woodland and as an occasional isolated specimen.

AKA Whitethorn, Quickthorn, Quick, May Bush.
Height 15 m, occasionally a tree.
Range Across Britain and Ireland except very wet, high or acid places.
ID Orange-brown bark cracking into rectangles, fluted on larger trees. Occasional long thorns on trunk. Characteristic small, lobed leaf; thorny shoots. White or pinkish-white flowers (p.240) develop into clusters of red 'haw' berries.

OTHER HAWTHORNS

There are cultivated hawthorn varieties, often with deep pink or double flowers. There is also the Glastonbury Thorn of mysterious origin, which flowers in winter, a few offspring of which exist in England. The **Midland Hawthorn**, *Crataegus oxyacanthoides* (**below**), is a rather rare woodland species in southern England with the leaf divided less than halfway to the base. It is difficult to distinguish because it hybridises readily with the common Hawthorn (p.153). Two American hybrids – Hybrid Cockspur Thorn, *C.* x *lavellei*, and Broad-leafed Cockspur Thorn, *C.* x *prunifolia* – have recently become fashionable as street trees and on housing estates, especially in England. They have a distinctive leaf with no lobes or indentations and large, brightly coloured fruit. The Azarole, *C. azarolus*, is a west Asian species, also with large red or yellow fruit, but a slightly lobed leaf. It is a very common street tree of southern Europe, but rather uncommon in Britain and Ireland.

MEDLAR *Mespilus germanica*

 This Asian species has naturalised in woods and hedges in parts of Europe, probably including England, and used to be much more popular in English and Irish orchards. It is known to hybridise with Hawthorn (p.153), though it is in a separate genus.

Height	5 m, often smaller and shrubby.
Range	Large, old orchards. Sometimes cottage gardens, very occasionally naturalised.
ID	Unmistakable, hard, green-brown fruit, round, with a flat, hairy base. Untidy, spiky profile, sometimes with thorns. Narrow, dull green leaf, wrinkled and leathery, with very short stalk. Large white flower (p.240), like a large Apple blossom.

ROWAN *Sorbus aucuparia*

 An elegant tree that is common throughout
Europe. In Britain and Ireland it is found
scattered thinly in mixed woodland and scrub,
becoming dominant at high altitudes, and on some
poor soils in groves and as individual specimens.

AKA Mountain Ash
Height 20 m.
Range Wild: mixed woodland and scrub, at high altitude
and sometimes on poor soils. Cultivated: streets,
parks, gardens.
ID Grey bark, becoming dark and ridged with age.
Pinnate leaf like Ash (p.224). Dense clusters of
cream flowers (p.241) develop into bright scarlet
berries.

Other Rowans

There are various cultivated varieties of the common Rowan (opposite) with ornamental profiles, bark, leaves and berries. In addition there are over 80 true species from around the world, but only the **Hupeh Rowan**, *Sorbus hupehensis* (**below**), is commonly planted in parks and gardens. It has a white or pink berry and a small, silvery, grey-green leaf. *Sorbus* 'Joseph Rock', a cultivated variety of the Hupeh Rowan with yellow berries and good autumn colours, has also become popular.

TRUE SERVICE TREE *Sorbus domestica*

Sorbus is a large and rather confusing genus, but the rowans and the True Service Tree are the only full species with pinnate leaves like Ash (p.224). The True Service Tree is probably a native of England, but is much commoner in continental Europe where it was originally grown for its fruit.

Height 20 m.

Range Occasional in parks and large gardens in England. One or two possibly wild woodland specimens.

ID Fruit like bunches of small apples or pears in shape and colour. Stouter profile and larger leaf than Rowan (p.156). Creamy flowers in bunches. Finely cracked bark, a mixture of oranges and dark brown.

WILD SERVICE TREE *Sorbus torminalis*

This rather uncommon small wild tree has a leaf like a maple and is often wrongly identified as a member of this family. The Wild Service Tree carries its leaves alternately on the shoot, while they are opposite each other in all the maples. No other *Sorbus* has a similar leaf.

AKA Checker or Chequer.
Height 20 m.
Range Individually scattered through woodland (often oak), in glades or on woodland edges. Even less common in gardens and as a street tree. S England, N to Lincolnshire.
ID Leaf shape and position. White flower (p.241) and brown fruit, quite unlike any maple. Scaly brown and grey bark.

WHITEBEAM *Sorbus aria*

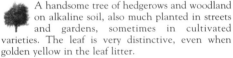 A handsome tree of hedgerows and woodland on alkaline soil, also much planted in streets and gardens, sometimes in cultivated varieties. The leaf is very distinctive, even when golden yellow in the leaf litter.

Height 20 m, often a many-stemmed shrub in woodland.
Range Native to S England and native or naturalised in mid-W Ireland. Common in streets, parks and gardens everywhere.
ID Leaf matt green above, but contrasting very pale silvery-white and hairy below, oval and toothed but not lobed. White flower (p.242), red fruit.

SWEDISH WHITEBEAM *Sorbus intermedia*

A whitebeam that is native to the Baltic States, existing in a number of varieties and hybrids. The leaf distinguishes it from Whitebeam (opposite).

Height 15 m, often shrubby.

Range Throughout Britain and Ireland as a park and street tree, sometimes in gardens, occasionally naturalised in woods and scrub.

ID Leaf clearly and deeply lobed as well as toothed, grey beneath not white as in Whitebeam. Purple-grey bark, smooth except for wide, shallow cracks. White flowers in dense clusters. Glossy green fruit ripens to bright scarlet, up to 20 in a bunch, larger than most related species.

OTHER WHITEBEAMS

The whitebeams are a fairly large and rather complicated group, most of which are not trees. The confusion has been increased by some botanists, who have described rare local populations and named them as species or subspecies, and also because whitebeams hybridise readily. The two most commonly planted hybrids are:

Broad-leaved Whitebeam or Service Tree of Fontainebleau, *Sorbus x latifolia*, existing as a natural hybrid in continental Europe where it has been described as a species with a number of Latin names. It is planted in Britain and Ireland as a cultivated hybrid and has shallow leaf lobes and a yellow-brown fruit.

Bastard Service Tree, *S. x hybrida* (**opposite**), with many other Latin names describing slight geographical variations. Probably a naturally occurring hybrid between Rowan (p.156) and Whitebeam (p.160), it has a red fruit and a leaf that is pinnate like Rowan at the base combined with the entire Whitebeam at the tip.

Another interesting species is Irish Whitebeam, *S. hibernica*, which is probably a local variety of Whitebeam and is endemic to Ireland – in other words, it is not found anywhere else in the world.

SNOWY MESPIL *Amelanchier laevis*

Of uncertain origin, Snowy Mespil is grown as an ornamental, mostly in southern England, for its fine autumn colour and especially for its spectacular, but short-lived, blossom.

Height Occasionally a tree to 12 m, often a shrub.

Range Common in English gardens, sometimes naturalised on heaths in S England, occasional in gardens elsewhere.

ID Shield-shaped, serrated leaf, rather like Apple (opposite), opens copper coloured, turns green in summer, deep red in autumn. Greenish-white flower with long petals, carried on long spikes. Fruit size of small haw, matures blackish purple, popular with birds. Smooth, dark grey bark.

CULTIVATED APPLE *Malus domestica syn. pumila*

 Even though apple trees are very familiar, there are so many hybrids and cultivated varieties, some quite different from each other, that a whole, large book is required to distinguish them. Cultivated Apple has also naturalised in the countryside, usually along roadsides or around abandoned houses and farms and usually in a degenerate form that can be confused with Crab Apple (p.166).

Height 2–10 m, depending on variety and rootstock.
Range Gardens and orchards, also naturalised in hedges and woods.
ID Leaf always woolly below. Fruit red, green, yellow, or a mixture of these, on hairy stalk. White or pink flower. Bark variable, usually grey or brown, cracked when old.

CRAB APPLE *Malus sylvestris*

An uncommon native tree posing two problems: firstly, distinguishing it from exotic species and cultivated varieties (see opposite), and secondly, distinguishing it from naturalised and degenerate Cultivated Apples (p.165).

Height 10 m, often smaller in hedges.
Range Thinly scattered in woods and hedges across Britain and Ireland, except on very acid soils.
ID Mature leaf never woolly below, shield-shaped or oval, sometimes irregular. Small, green fruit, speckled with red when ripe, on hairless stalk. Large, flat, white flower, sometimes flushed very pale pink, never deep pink. Brown, cracked bark.

OTHER CRAB APPLES

There are about 25 species of crab apple worldwide and countless cultivated varieties bred for ornament, as pollinators in orchards and, occasionally, for fruit. The two species most commonly found as street trees or in gardens are Japanese Crab, *Malus floribunda*, a stocky tree grown for its profuse, single flowers that are red in bud, open pink and fade to white; and **Hupeh Crab**, M. *hupehensis*, a tall, fast-growing tree, increasingly planted for its pure white blossom and its fruit, ripening from yellow and orange to deep red-purple (**below**).

The three commonest ornamental varieties, also used as pollinators in commercial orchards, are *Malus* 'Golden Hornet', a small, white-blossomed hybrid that bears masses of long, golden fruits along its branches; *Malus* 'John Downie', a large white-blossomed hybrid that bears spectacular bunches of scarlet and orange fruit; and Purple Crab, M. x *purpurea*, an untidy looking hybrid often planted in streets, around buildings and in gardens for its red-purple leaves, red blossom and small red or purple apples.

QUINCE *Cydonia oblonga*

 The Quince is a fruit that has declined in popularity. It is a small tree found in old orchards, or occasionally in smaller gardens as a specimen tree growing in a lawn.

Height 5 m.
Range Large, old orchards or occasional garden specimen.
ID Short, dull, oval leaf with red veins and characteristic white fluff below. Odd, domed profile and twisted branches. Pale pink flower. Large, fragrant, yellow-green fruit, usually oblong. Grey bark.

COMMON PEAR *Pyrus communis*

 There are many cultivated varieties of pear and a European wild tree that is doubtfully native in Britain and Ireland. The main differences lie in the fruit, though some cultivated varieties have longer leaves.

Height 15 m.

Range Wild or naturalised, sometimes as degenerate cultivated variety, thinly scattered in hedges and woodland. Cultivated in gardens and orchards.

ID Straggling profile, looks distinctly spiky in winter. Very shiny leaf, shape varies, only hairy below when first opens. White flower with purple anthers; often appears in March. Fruit varies; small, hard and rather round in wild. Dark, cracked bark, often with square plates when old.

169

PLYMOUTH PEAR *Pyrus cordata*

A very rare native tree found in Devon and Cornwall and also in Brittany. This is probably Britain's rarest and most endangered tree and there are various current projects to study and preserve it.

AKA	Wild Pear (incorrectly, as can be confused with wild form of Common Pear, p.169).
Height	8 m.
Range	A few wild specimens around Plymouth in Devon. Another, possibly separate, species or subspecies in Cornwall. Some in gardens and collections.
ID	Pointed flowerhead with small, foul-smelling flowers. Small, round, green, fruit ripens reddish and is rather haw-shaped. Bark and profile similar to Hawthorn (p.153).

WILLOW-LEAVED PEAR *Pyrus salicifolia*

 A small ornamental tree that has recently become very popular. Because it is usually weeping in form and has long, thin leaves it is often misidentified as a willow.

Height 8 m.
Range Gardens and parks, commonest in S England.
ID Long, narrow leaf, silvery at first, turning dark and gloss-green. White flower. Fruit like a pear, but very small (2–3 cm).

Myrobalan Plum *Prunus cerasifera*

A Balkan species with two cultivated varieties 'Atropurpurea' (also known as *Prunus pissardii*) and 'Nigra', often planted for their blossom and leaves. The wild form is often mistaken for Blackthorn (opposite) but it is usually much larger, more tree-like, and blossoms four to six weeks earlier.

AKA Cherry Plum.

Height 8 m.

Range Wild form naturalised in S England. Ornamentals common in parks and gardens.

ID White or pale pink flower, sometimes double, appears February/March. Fruit, a small green plum, ripens to red, seldom sets in Britain. Dark bark. Leaf green in wild form; red maturing to purple-brown in cultivated forms.

BLACKTHORN *Prunus spinosa*

The commonest wild plum in Europe and the only one native to Britain and Ireland, Blackthorn is usually a shrub in scrubland or hedges. Sometimes it grows in groves of single-trunked plants forming a canopy and spreading by root suckers – the only time it is really a tree.

AKA	Sloe.
Height	5 m, usually smaller and shrubby.
Range	Everywhere except very difficult soils: scrubland, hedgerows, sometimes in mixed woods or as large groves.
ID	Dark bark; black, thorny shoots, covered in dense clouds of small white flowers in early April (p.242), before leaves. Purple fruit, called sloes, ripen late but remain bitter. Upright profile.

173

CULTIVATED PLUM *Prunus domestica*

Plums have been cultivated for a long time and there is disagreement about whether they originate from a true species or a hybrid. Some experts designate the varieties with thorns as a subspecies called *institia*. They sometimes naturalise in the wild, for example a form with large purple fruits in south-east Ireland.

AKA Gage, Prune.
Height 10 m.
Range Orchards and gardens, occasionally naturalised.
ID Untidy profile. Toothed leaf variable, shiny on top. Fruit variable in size, shape and colour – green, yellow, orange, red, purple, or a combination. Reddish young shoots; white flowers (p.243).

OTHER PLUMS

The exact classification of plums is complicated because they have been cultivated for a very long time, they hybridise easily and naturalise quite frequently. The **Damson (below)** is a Cultivated Plum (see opposite) with small purple fruits that are sometimes round and sometimes oval. It is particularly hardy and is often grown as a wind-break around orchards. It naturalises readily and is a fairly common hedgerow species in the English Midlands. The Bullace is a similar plant, commonest in southern England, with fruits intermediate between the Damson and the Blackthorn (p.173) – it may be a hybrid or back-cross between these two, but this is uncertain. A similar, unnamed, thorny plum with small fruits that ripen yellow-green is found in Ireland.

ALMOND *Prunus dulcis*

A west Asian species that naturalises in a thorny form in the Middle East, North Africa and southern Europe and is important for its seeds. The Sweet Almond variety is used in confectionery, the Bitter Almond variety for medicine and perfume. In Britain and Ireland it is usually an early flowering ornamental, with several cultivated varieties, though the seed ripens well in milder parts.

Height 8 m.

Range Parks, suburban gardens and often as a street tree in milder parts.

ID Large, early flower, sometimes double, in shades of pink and white (p.243). Dark bark. Large, dull leaf hangs down. Hard, flattened, hairy green fruit contains wrinkled nut.

APRICOT *Prunus armeniaca*

 A small tree originating in the Orient and important as an orchard crop in southern Europe. It is quite frost hardy, but flowers in March and fruits in July in Britain and Ireland, so it is normally grown against a south-facing wall or, increasingly, in conservatories. It is particularly suitable for this as the long, supple shoots train very easily.

Height 5 m.

Range Walled gardens and conservatories in Britain and Ireland, sometimes as free-standing specimen.

ID Large, long-stalked, finely toothed, oval leaf. Distinctively pink flowers (p.244) appear before leaves; unmistakable orange-yellow hairy fruit.

177

PEACH AND NECTARINE *Prunus persica*

Peaches are an important fruit crop throughout much of the world with many cultivated varieties. The Nectarine is an increasingly popular variety with a fruit like a small peach with smooth rather than hairy skin. In Britain and Ireland peaches will survive without protection, but seldom produce fruit, so are usually grown under shelter.

Height 8 m.

Range Normally against walls or under glass in Britain and Ireland.

ID Long, narrow leaf like Almond (p.176), but broadest above the middle. Flowers (p.244) darker pink than Apricot (pp.177 and 244) and appear later, with first leaves. Fruit variable in size and shape, usually red, pink and yellow.

Japanese Flowering Cherries *Prunus serrulata*

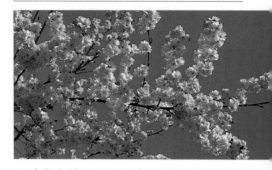

Probably originating from China, this species was developed at an early date in Japan and, later, by European plant breeders. Today it exists in more cultivated varieties than any other ornamental tree; some have been described as separate species, but this is now frowned on. The leaf identifies the species; to distinguish one variety from another requires a specialist book.

Height 5–12 m, depending on variety.
Range Common in gardens, parks, and as street trees.
ID Big, sharply toothed leaf, pale gold and pink in autumn. Copper or bronze foliage in some varieties. Flowers single or double, in shades of pink, white or greenish-yellow. Profile varies from weeping to narrow, upright column; some dwarf forms.

WILD CHERRY *Prunus avium*

A splendid tree native to Britain and Ireland though nowhere common in the wild. It often occurs as a grove of root suckers from one parent. The cherries are seldom seen because birds take them. There is also a double-flowered cultivated variety.

AKA	Gean, Mazzard.
Height	25 m.
Range	Wild: woods and hedges. Cultivated: parks, gardens and streets everywhere.
ID	Upright profile. Leaf opens bronze, turns green, hangs limply from prominent knob on stalk. Smooth, shiny, purple-grey bark, peels in horizontal bands. Large, long-stalked, cup-shaped, white flower in clusters in April. Fruit small, red cherry.

BIRD CHERRY *Prunus padus*

This species is confused with Wild Cherry (opposite), mainly because *Prunus avium*, the Latin name of Wild Cherry, translates as Bird Cherry. It is native to north Britain and Ireland, usually on limestone and often by water. It is frequently planted everywhere, sometimes in 'improved' ornamental varieties.

Height 15 m, usually smaller.
Range Wild: open wood or woodland edges. Cultivated: gardens, parks and road verges everywhere.
ID Leaf pale on red stalk. Smooth, dark, aromatic bark, with prominent orange flecks. Small white flower and small green fruit ripening red, both on long spikes not clusters. Small, bushy profile.

OTHER CHERRIES

The Sour Cherry, *Prunus cerasus*, is uncommon in Britain and Ireland except in the ornamental form 'Rhexii', which has ball-shaped, white, many-petalled flowers appearing late in the spring. The tree is also important for being one parent of most of the hybrid cherries that are cultivated for fruit.

The **Black Cherry**, *P. serotina* (**below**), is a North American species with dense spikes of smaller flowers and purplish-black fruit. It is sometimes planted and occasionally naturalised in Britain and Ireland.

There are a few other exotic species that are rarely seen, and many cultivated varieties and hybrids grown both for fruit and for ornament.

CHERRY LAUREL *Prunus laurocerasus*

A poisonous shrub from the Near East, much planted in estates and large gardens as hedging, to line avenues and as game coverts. It is also quite commonly naturalised as woodland understorey in western Britain. In wetter parts of Ireland and west Britain it sometimes makes a single-trunked tree.

Height   Occasionally to 15 m, commonly a spreading shrub.
Range   Estates and large gardens throughout Ireland and Britain, commonest in W.
  ID   Evergreen leaf similar to Rhododendron (p.220). Insignificant white-green flower on short spike (p.245). Distinctive oval fruit, ripens like small black cherry. Grey-brown bark with horizontal banding.

PORTUGAL LAUREL *Prunus lusitanica*

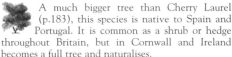 A much bigger tree than Cherry Laurel (p.183), this species is native to Spain and Portugal. It is common as a shrub or hedge throughout Britain, but in Cornwall and Ireland becomes a full tree and naturalises.

Height Sometimes to 20 m in extreme W, commonly smaller.

Range Everywhere as a shrub, Cornwall and Ireland as a tree.

ID Leathery, evergreen leaf on long, red stalk. Small, fragrant cream-white flower in dense spikes in mid-June (p.245). Small, red berry, a few maturing to black. Black bark, smooth or slightly scaly.

COMMON LABURNUM *Laburnum anagyroides*

A small poisonous tree from central and southern Europe that is commonly planted in England, Wales and Ireland for its spectacular flowers. It is largely replaced in Scotland by Scotch Laburnum (p.186) and in modern planting by Voss's Laburnum (p.187).

Height 10 m.

Range Common in urban gardens, parks and streets, especially as older tree. Sometimes naturalised.

ID Yellow, pea-like flower in long, drooping sprays. Pea-like seed pod explodes open spreading poisonous seeds. Smooth brownish-green bark, browner with orange flakes when old. Compound leaf with three leaflets. Blue-green, slightly hairy shoot.

SCOTCH LABURNUM *Laburnum alpinum*

With much the same native range as Common Laburnum (p.185), Scotch Laburnum is found at higher altitudes. It tends to replace the common species in Scottish plantings and has more resistance to cold. The two species and one hybrid (see opposite) can be hard to distinguish.

AKA Alpine Laburnum.
Height 10 m.
Range Gardens, parks and road verges in Scotland. Uncommon elsewhere in Britain and Ireland.
ID Yellow, pea-like flower, smaller and in longer spikes than Common Laburnum, opening a couple of weeks later (usually late June). Larger leaves and hairless shoots. Pod with winged upper seam.

Hybrid Laburnums

Voss's Laburnum, *Laburnum* x *watereri* syn. *L. vossii* syn. *L. parkesii*, is a hybrid between Common Laburnum (p.185) and Scotch Laburnum (opposite). It is by far the commonest laburnum planted recently, because it has the large flowers of one parent and the long flower spike of the other. It is also more densely leaved and produces much fewer poisonous seeds.

Adam's Laburnum, +*Laburnocytisus adamii* syn. *Laburnum adami* (**below**), is an extraordinary botanical oddity that was a popular Victorian conversation piece and is still found in some parks and gardens. It is a graft hybrid between the Common Laburnum and a totally unrelated dwarf shrub called Purple Broom, developed by an eccentric Parisian gardener. It bears leaves and flowers of both its dissimilar parents, together with leaves and flowers that are combinations of the two.

MIMOSA *Acacia dealbata*

The acacias are a large group but the Mimosa from Australia is the only one that is hardy in Britain and Ireland. This hardiness is variable; it grows happily at 300 m altitude in the Wicklow Mountains with considerable winter snow, but suffers from frost-burn in much of England.

AKA Silver Wattle.
Height 15 m.
Range Larger gardens in Devon, Cornwall, the Isle of Wight and Ireland. Occasional in sheltered gardens elsewhere.
ID Very delicate, feathery, silver-green leaf. Globes of yellow flowers early in the year. Smooth bark, bright blue-green when young, darkens with age. Flat brown seed pod.

JUDAS TREE Cercis siliquastrum

A south European tree grown in parks and gardens in southern and eastern England. There is a cultivated variety with white flowers.

Height 10 m.

Range Relatively common in parks and gardens in S and E England, rare in rest of Britain and Ireland.

ID Large, heart-shaped leaf; long, bean-like seed pod. Pink, pea-like flowers, often in unexpected places on branches and trunk. Bark purplish when young, dull grey-pink with age.

LOCUST TREE *Robinia pseudoacacia*

This poisonous North American tree has naturalised in parts of continental Europe. It resists air pollution well and likes lighter soils. A thornless form grafted on a standard stock is sometimes used as a street tree. The name Locust Tree is confusing as it is also used for the Carob, *Ceratonia siliqua*, an important southern European crop.

AKA False Acacia, Robinia, Black Locust.

Height To 30 m, usually smaller.

Range Common in urban streets, parks and gardens in S England; less common elsewhere.

ID 3 to 10 leaflets on a stalk. Reddish shoot with paired spines. Hanging spikes of white flowers. Flattened seed pod. Smooth bark, rich brown when young, going grey.

HONEY LOCUST *Gleditsia triacanthus*

A tree from the American mid-west with bunches of ferocious spines, up to 30 cm long, on its trunk. Unfortunately a spineless cultivated variety called 'Inermis' is sometimes planted, confusing identification.

Height 20 m.

Range Streets, parks and gardens in S and E England. Not as common as Locust Tree (opposite).

ID Spines on trunk (p.246), but one variety without. Yellow-green leaf, pinnate like Ash (p.224), with about 20 leaflets on a stalk. Pale yellow-green male and female flowers, on separate spikes at same time. Seed ripens to brown, uncommon in Britain and Ireland. Dark, ridged bark.

PAGODA TREE *Sophora japonica*

An oriental species grown for its foliage, attractive flowers and graceful profile. It is often confused with the rather similar and much commoner Locust Tree (p.190).

AKA Scholar's Tree.
Height 20 m.
Range Scattered in more sheltered gardens, commonest in S England.
ID Blue-green shoot turns green and smooth. No spines. Narrower leaf than Locust Tree. White pea-flower only in very hot summers on trees over 30 years old.

TREE OF HEAVEN *Ailanthus altissima*

 A fine Chinese tree that is quite common in towns as it withstands air pollution. It resembles Ash (p.224).

AKA Swingle.

Height 25 m.

Range Common in streets, squares and parks in London; often in larger gardens in S and E England. Uncommon rest of Britain and Ireland.

ID Leaf opens late, like Ash but much larger leaf and leaflets, toothed at base only, with foul smell when crushed. Distinctive, fat orange shoot with leaf scars like Horse Chestnut (pp. 205 and 247). Smooth dark bark, with streaks. Red bud; cream flower in early July. Winged seed, ripens bright red on one side.

BOX *Buxus sempervirens*

Well known as a hedging plant, often heavily trimmed and low, this slow-growing poisonous evergreen also forms bushes and thickets in game coverts and sometimes a full-sized tree. The leaf can only be confused with another hedging plant, *Lonicera*, which has smaller, paler, less waxy foliage and never forms a true tree.

Height Occasionally to 8 m.

Range Probably native to a few places in S England, widely planted everywhere as hedge or trimmed shrub. Sometimes naturalised in woods.

ID Pale brown bark, weathers to grey. Tree profile twisted and leaning. Small leaf, dark green above, paler below. Yellow-green flower; blue-green 3-horned fruit.

STAG'S HORN SUMAC *Rhus typhina*

 A popular garden tree from the USA that takes its English name from the peculiar pattern of its branches, arranged like antlers. It is usually surrounded by root suckers, often some distance from the tree.

Height 10 m.
Range Gardens, commonest in Ireland.
ID Thick, hairy shoots. Delicate pinnate leaves, like Ash (p.224), with serrated leaflets turning bright gold and orange in autumn, as shown above. Fruit an odd upright cluster of hairy, purple berries.

HOLLY *Ilex aquifolium*

A very familiar tree, but the leaves may be spineless, and it can then be confusing. There are also cultivated varieties, mostly with variegated or coloured leaves. Native to most of Europe and all of Britain and Ireland except extreme northern Scotland, it is declining due to Christmas over-exploitation of female trees for their berries.

Height Occasionally to 20 m in S England.

Range Wild as understorey in oak or mixed woods, sometimes as isolated groves on hillsides. Much planted in hedges, gardens and wind-breaks.

ID Crinkled, spiny, shiny green leaf, but varies, may be spineless. Green berry (females only) in clusters, ripens to scarlet. Smooth pinkish-grey bark, dull silvery-grey with warts when old.

NORWAY MAPLE *Acer platanoides*

A fine tree native to most of Europe, but introduced into Britain and Ireland where it is commoner than is realised. It is most often mistaken for Sycamore (p.199). There are many cultivated varieties, most having been 'improved' by variegated or odd-coloured foliage.

Height 25 m.

Range Common in gardens, wind-breaks, parks and road verges in S England. Less common rest of Britain and Ireland. Sometimes naturalised.

ID Leaf has 5 lobes, tipped with fine points, extra points on shoulders. Distinctive gold flower opens early, before leaves. Red-brown terminal bud; double-winged seed. Smooth, grey bark. Domed profile; short, unbranched trunk.

FIELD MAPLE *Acer campestre*

This small-leaved maple is the only native member of the family, though its native range is confined to southern England and it does not like acid soils. It is commoner as a hedgerow species in lowland areas than as a tree, though it can grow quite big.

Height Occasionally to 25 m.

Range Common in England as far N as the Midlands. Rare and always planted elsewhere.

ID Profile often lopsided. Small, deep green leaf has 5 (sometimes 3) lobes. Fissured, grey-brown bark, flaking with orange underneath. Slightly hairy, corky shoot. Yellow-green flowers in sparse upright clusters in May. Seeds have 2 wings almost in a straight line.

SYCAMORE *Acer pseudoplatanus*

This native of central European uplands was an early introduction to Britain and Ireland. It naturalised well and is now one of the commonest broad-leaved trees in town and countryside. It also thrives on very exposed coasts, islands and mountains in Scotland and W Ireland.

AKA Great Maple; in Scotland (incorrectly) Plane.
Height 35 m.
Range Everywhere there are trees.
ID Leaf has 5 pointed and toothed lobes, often with black fungus blotches and small red galls. Stout shoot with fat, green buds. Smooth grey bark like Beech (p.123), cracks into squares with age. Yellow-green flower in long, open spikes in April. Double-winged seeds in clusters.

SMOOTH JAPANESE MAPLE *Acer palmatum*

 A popular ornamental species introduced into Britain and Ireland about 200 years ago. It also has cultivated varieties with coloured leaves, bark or shoots. Its main attraction is the delicate leaf with glorious autumn colours. The closely related Downy Japanese Maple, *Acer japonicum*, is smaller, with leaves covered in downy hairs when they open.

Height 15 m.
Range Gardens, some parks.
ID Leaf varies with 5–7 long, serrated lobes. Smooth bark, striped in shades of brown, greying with age. Slender shoot, red above, bright green below. Purple-pink flowers in small clusters. Double-winged seeds. Tall domed profile with short trunk.

Paper Bark Maple *Acer griseum*

 A Chinese species that is becoming increasingly popular in British and Irish gardens.

Height 10 m.

Range Gardens.

ID Rich, chestnut-coloured bark, peels away sideways in sheets to reveal smooth areas of trunk, branches and twigs (p.246). Distinctive 3-lobed leaf unfolds orange, buff and brown, becomes dark green in summer, turns deep red in autumn as shown above. Green-yellow flower, hangs in small bunches. Large seed, wings nearly parallel. Slender, open profile with ascending branches.

SNAKE-BARK MAPLES

Snake-bark Maples have distinctive striped and patterned bark. There are several species and cultivated varieties, so they are difficult to distinguish, compounded by the fact that the botanists and horticulturists who originally described them were themselves confused. A specialist book may be needed for precise identification. The commonest full species are:

Père David's Maple, *Acer davidii*, with smooth, olive-green bark divided by blue-white lines (**below**).

Grey-budded Snake-bark Maple, *A. rufinerve*, normally with green bark with greyish white stripes, sometimes grey bark with pink stripes.

Hers's Maple, *A. hersii*, with olive-green bark with white stripes tinged with green.

Red Snake-bark Maple, *A. capillipes*, with bright green bark, striped bright white.

OTHER MAPLES

Most of the large Maple family grow well in the north European climate and it has been fashionable for landowners to collect them. The commonest of the many other species are:

Cappadocian Maple, *Acer cappadocicum*, which has an unusual leaf shape, produces suckers and has both yellow- and red-leaved varieties.

Montpelier Maple, *A. monspessulanum*, which is native to south and central Europe, and resembles Field Maple (p.198), but with three leaf lobes and a distinctive seed.

Italian Maple, *A. opalus*, another European tree, similar to Sycamore (p.199) with a smaller, shallower lobed leaf and a tighter angle between the seed wings.

Sugar Maple, *A. saccharum*, which is often confused with Norway Maple (p.197), but its leaf lobes have a wedge-shaped base (**overleaf**).

Amur Maple, *A. ginnala*, a small garden species with a distinctive leaf in which the centre lobe is much longer than the other two.

Red Maple, *A. rubrum*, with leaves that are only lobed at the end and are silvery underneath.

Silver Maple, *A. saccharinum*, also with leaves that are silvery underneath, but they are quite a different shape – the lobes have smaller lobes on them with fine, tapering points.

Ash-leafed Maple or Box-elder, *A. negundo*, with a distinctive leaf like Ash (p.224) or Elder (p.228), usually planted in a variegated form.

Sugar Maple leaf (see p.203)

HORSE CHESTNUT *Aesculus hippocastanum*

A familiar tree from south-east Europe, introduced early into Britain and widely planted and naturalised. Its fruit is the well-known conker. A hybrid form with pink flowers makes a much smaller tree.

Height 35 m.

Range Planted and naturalised in town and countryside, commoner in England and Wales than in Scotland and Ireland.

ID Large leaf with 5–7 unstalked leaflets. Large, sticky bud (p.247). Large upright flowers, in white candle-like clusters with pink spots (p.247). Fruit is green spiked shell with 1–3 shiny brown inedible nuts inside. Rough bark, breaking off in long plates. Spreading profile.

SPINDLE *Euonymus europaeus*

Normally a native shrub of scrubland on chalk and limestone, the Spindle sometimes makes a small, straggly tree. Its hard timber was originally used to make spindles for spinning wool. A non-native species, Broad-leaved Spindle, *Euonymus latifolius*, is sometimes planted, and has longer and much broader leaves.

AKA	Pegwood.
Height	6 m, commonly a smaller, many-stemmed shrub.
Range	Scrubland, woodland edges and hedgerows on alkaline soil in lowland Britain and Ireland.
ID	Unmistakable, bright orange, eared fruit (p.248). Inconspicuous greenish-white flower. Grey-green bark; four-sided shoot. Oval, pointed, bright green leaf in opposite pairs.

BUCKTHORN *Rhamnus catharticus*

Normally a native shrub of scrubland, woodland understorey and hedgerows, Buckthorn may reach tree height, but usually has a many-stemmed shrub profile. It prefers limy soils, but is quite adaptable. It can be confused with Alder Buckthorn (p.208).

Height 6 m, usually smaller.
Range Commonest in lowland areas with dry, non-acidic soils. Rare in Ireland, absent from Scotland.
ID Orange-brown scaly bark, sometimes with spines on trunk. Leaf on long stalk, with 2–4 pairs of prominent, spreading veins, turns yellow-brown in autumn. Inconspicuous white-green male (p.248) and female flower. Poisonous currant-like berry, ripens glossy black in autumn.

ALDER BUCKTHORN *Frangula alnus*

This is neither an alder nor a buckthorn, but the leaf resembles an alder and the whole plant is often confused with Buckthorn (p.207). It has the profile of a small, bushy tree, and prefers moist, acid conditions.

AKA	Black Dogwood.
Height	Occasionally to 6 m.
Range	Isolated populations in England, Wales and Ireland, absent from Scotland.
ID	Smooth, finely cracked bark with no thorns. Shield-shaped, yellow-green leaf on short stalk with 7–8 pairs of veins, turns bright yellow in autumn. Tiny green-white flowers in small clusters at branch tips. Green currant-like berry ripens through red to glossy black.

SMALL-LEAVED LIME *Tilia cordata*

A scattered native of England and Wales, where it is not known to propagate from seed. The 3 common species of lime are difficult to distinguish; despite the English names, leaf size is not reliable – the underside is a better guide.

AKA	Linden Tree (used for all limes).
Height	30 m.
Range	Wild on limestone in England and Wales. Everywhere in parks and larger gardens.
ID	Heart-shaped leaf, pale blue-green and smooth below, the only hairs being small, in orange-brown tufts at joints of veins. Fragrant white and green flowers in bunches in early July (p.249). Fruit in clusters of small, hairless, unribbed yellow-green balls.

LARGE-LEAVED LIME *Tilia platyphyllos*

Probably a native in some limestone areas of England and Wales. It is very similar to Small-leaved Lime (p.209) and there are a couple of cultivated varieties with coloured shoots or fancy leaves.

AKA Linden Tree (used for all limes).
Height 30 m.
Range Isolated specimens in mixed woods in England and E Wales. Everywhere in streets, parks, avenues and larger gardens.
ID Heart-shaped leaf, both sides same colour; hairy below, sometimes above; hairy leaf stalks and twigs. Yellow-white flower in late June. Fruit hairy green ball with five ribs. Finely cracked, dark grey bark.

COMMON LIME *Tilia x europaea* syn. *T. vulgaris*

A natural hybrid of Small-leaved Lime (p.209) and Large-leaved Lime (opposite) that may be native in England. It is the tallest and commonest lime in Britain and Ireland.

AKA Linden Tree (used for all limes).

Height 40 m. This species is frequently pollarded.

Range Common in streets and avenues; specimen in parks, gardens, churchyards, village greens.

ID Leaf paler below than above, hairless with some pale tufts in main vein joints. Dense shoots from bosses on trunk and at base of tree, often mixed with root suckers. Smooth, dull grey bark, develops fine cracks with age. Yellow-white flower hangs in small clusters in early July. Slightly oval, faintly ribbed, hairy fruit.

PITTOSPORUM *Pittosporum tenuifolium*

Pittosporums are small trees from Australasia, the Far East and South Africa of which two species are fairly common in Cornwall and Ireland. *Pittosporum tenuifolium* is the commonest, with its foliage often in florist's shops, while *P. tobira* is less common. There are cultivated varieties with cream-variegated or silver leaves.

Height 15 m, usually smaller.

Range Common in coastal gardens in Cornwall and Ireland, rare elsewhere.

ID *P. tenuifolium*: deeply waved, crinkled leaf, pale green with prominent white midrib. *P. tobira*: sparse, whorled leaf; rougher, darker bark. Both: small, fragrant, cup-shaped, dark purple flower in May. Green fruit ripens to black.

FRENCH TAMARISK *Tamarix gallica*

A distinctive coastal shrub that sometimes makes a tree. Native to the coasts of France and other European countries, it is probably introduced to Britain where it has a limited range on the southern coasts of England. It has been used to stabilise dry-stone walls in north Cornwall.

Height 10 m, usually smaller.
Range S coasts of England.
ID Tiny, fleshy, scale-like leaf. Shoot covered in a froth of pinkish-white flowers in late spring.

Orange Bark Myrtle *Myrtus apiculata*

A South American evergreen that is common in Ireland. It is rather rare in British gardens, being largely confined to the south-west.

Height   10 m.

Range   Gardens and shrubberies in Ireland, especially in the SW where it sometimes naturalises.

ID   Orange bark, flaking off finely to reveal white areas. Small, deep green leaf, similar to Box (p.194) with a small point on the end. Masses of four-petalled white flowers, open from red and green buds in late summer. Small berry, briefly red, turns black.

CIDER GUM *Eucalyptus gunnii*

Most of this large group of fast-growing, evergreen broad-leaves from Australasia are not hardy in Britain and Ireland. The young leaves are often used by florists. The Cider Gum is the commonest eucalyptus in Britain.

AKA   Latin name more common than English.
Height   35 m.
Range   Larger gardens.
ID   Pinkish-orange bark, peeling to reveal smooth grey. Small, shiny, blue-grey young leaf, aromatic and rounded, with no stalk. Spearhead-shaped old leaf, dark blue-grey above, yellowish-green below with a lot of prominent veins. White fluffy flowers in July. Top-shaped white seed with a flat end.

BLUE GUM *Eucalyptus globulus*

A common tree in Ireland, but rare in Britain. In high rainfall areas of south-west Ireland the Blue Gum sets speed records for growth – up to 3 m a year. The young leaves, as shown above, are often used as foliage colour in parks and public gardens.

Height 40 m+.
Range Gardens, estates, occasional road verges in Ireland. Rare in Britain.
ID Small, shiny, blue-grey young leaf, similar to Cider Gum (p.215), aromatic and rounded with no stalk. Distinctly sickle-shaped, deep blue-green old leaf. Colourful, variable bark in shades of grey, brown, pink and green, peels readily. Large, top-shaped dark fruit (p.249).

SNOW GUM *Eucalyptus niphophila*

 A slower growing eucalyptus that has recently gained popularity as a garden species in Britain because it is decorative and very hardy.

Height 25 m (most trees in cultivation are young).
Range Gardens, particularly in England.
ID Brilliant blue-white trunk and branches. Shoot bright yellow, then dark red, then violet. Leaf unusually adult from the first year: unfolds orange, turns brown, then grey-green; oval, with 3 parallel veins each side of midrib, and red margin. Spectacular pure white flower.

PRICKLY CASTOR OIL TREE *Kalopanax pictus*

A small garden tree from the Far East, mostly confined to places with a mild winter climate. There is a hybrid, 'Maximowiczii', and many intermediate forms. These strange, gaunt plants with spiny trunks look as though they belong in a hothouse.

Height 15 m, commonly smaller.
Range Gardens in S and W of Britain, commoner in Ireland.
ID Dull grey, ridged bark, warty and usually spiny. Leaf varies, like large, coarse, dark green maple leaf with prominent veins and white hairs below. Clusters of small white flowers, hang in tassels in late summer. Oval black fruit hangs on tree till mid-winter.

CORNELIAN CHERRY *Cornus mas*

 The Dogwood family contains many popular garden shrubs, but the Cornelian Cherry is the only common one that really deserves to be called a tree. It takes its name from its fruit, although it is mainly grown for its early flowers. A European native, it has been introduced to British and Irish gardens, often in a form with a variegated leaf.

Height 10 m, but often a shrub.
Range Gardens, occasionally naturalised on lime-rich soils.
ID Red, lozenge-shaped edible fruit. Bright yellow flower (p.250) on bare grey-green twig in early spring.

RHODODENDRON *Rhododendron ponticum*

This large and popular family of plants, shrubs and small trees is grown in collections in larger gardens. *Rhododendron ponticum* is a European species that has naturalised in Britain and Ireland, especially in western Scotland and western Ireland, in areas of high rainfall and acid soil. It is very invasive as a woodland understorey species, becoming a problem in some areas. Garden varieties and other species have flowers in a wide range of colours.

Height 10 m.
Range Gardens, hillsides and woodlands.
ID Spreading bells of purple-pink flowers. Long, dark-green, leathery leaf. Large, many-scaled bud. Grey, finely cracked bark. Shrubby, many-stemmed profile.

STRAWBERRY TREE *Arbutus unedo*

 A native tree of western Ireland. The Cyprus Strawberry Tree, *Arbutus andrachne*, is very rare in Britain and Ireland, but a hybrid of the two, *A. x andrachnoides*, with small fruit and very red bark is fairly frequent in large, old gardens in milder areas.

AKA Arbutus, Crankany.

Height 12 m.

Range Wild in W Ireland, particularly mid-Kerry. Gardens and parks in milder parts of Britain.

ID Very flaky, dark red bark, ages to grey. Bushy profile, often leaning or prone. Shiny, evergreen leaf on red stalk. Greenish-white flowers appear in autumn; edible strawberry-like fruits ripen to bright red at same time.

SNOWBELL TREE *Styrax japonica*

 An attractive, small, flowering tree from the Far East that is popular in gardens.

Height 10 m.
Range Larger gardens, mostly in England.
ID Fawn-coloured bark with pink stripes when young, ageing to grey with orange cracks. Pointed leaf, darker green above than below, usually cupped. Masses of white, bell-like bunches of flowers hang below branches in June. Long, smooth, greenish-grey fruit. Small, neatly rounded, rather dense profile.

LILAC *Syringa vulgaris*

A small flowering tree that is native in south-east Europe, common in gardens in Britain and Ireland, and is occasionally naturalised. The familiar cones of small tubular flowers in late spring have been bred in a number of shades of violet and blue as well as a common white form.

Height 7 m.

Range Gardens everywhere, sometimes on road verges or naturalised on wasteland.

ID Blue-grey bark, ridged with age. Arrowhead-shaped leaf, shiny green or yellow-green above, dull below; size differs with variety.

ASH *Fraxinus excelsior*

A fine native tree that has become the dominant tall species on alkaline land since Dutch Elm disease, and is often haphazardly pollarded. There are some exotic species and cultivated varieties, notably a weeping form.

Height 40 m.

Range Everywhere in Britain and Ireland in town and countryside where the soil is not too acid.

ID Smooth bark, thick and ridged with age. Leaf with central stem and about 10 toothed leaflets, appearing very late in spring. Distinctive winter shoot, grey-green with squat black buds. Flowers vary, usually yellow, white or pale green, in bunches. Single-winged 'ash-key' seeds (p.250).

MANNA ASH *Fraxinus ornus*

 A small tree native to south-east Europe that has become popular in Britain and Ireland.

AKA Flowering Ash.

Height 20 m.

Range Parks, road verges and gardens, commonest in S England.

ID Striking bunches of creamy-white, fragrant flowers hang from branches in late spring (p.251). Very smooth, dark bark. Leaf has fewer and larger leaflets on longer stalks than native Ash (opposite); slimmer seed wings.

225

FOXGLOVE TREE *Paulownia tomentosa*

An Oriental tree that is frost hardy, but does not flower well in the north of Britain and Ireland. In winter it can be confused with the Indian Bean Tree (opposite), but it has much smoother bark.

Height 20 m.
Range Larger gardens, mostly in S England and S Ireland.
ID Gaunt, untidy profile. Tubular, violet flower, appears before leaves in early summer, with slight resemblance to a foxglove. Large, drooping, hairy, heart-shaped leaf, with a long point on the end, and usually a point halfway down each side. Sticky, beaked, glossy white-green fruit.

INDIAN BEAN TREE *Catalpa bignonioides*

 An American flowering tree, quite common in gardens in southern England, but unusual elsewhere in Britain and Ireland. It is usually the last tree to break bud, sometimes as late as June. It has extraordinary seed pods up to 40 cm long, which dangle from the tree all winter. There are some ornamental forms and hybrids.

AKA Red Indian Bean Tree.
Height 15 m.
Range Gardens in S England. Very occasionally naturalised; uncommon elsewhere.
ID Leaves late, variable, but usually pear-shaped and foul smelling if crushed. Distinctive white flower with coloured spots (p.251), rather like Horse Chestnut (pp. 205 and 247). Rough, scaly bark.

ELDER *Sambucus nigra*

A very common native shrub and small tree in hedges, scrub and wasteland, also found in woodland understorey. There are some ornamental varieties with variegated or fancy-shaped leaves. A red-berried species from Scandinavia, *Sambucus racemosa*, is naturalised in Scotland.

Height 8 m, often a shrub.
Range Everywhere, particularly in hedgerows.
ID Smooth, spotted young bark; fawn-coloured and deeply furrowed with age. Soft, pithy young branches; mature wood very hard. Serrated leaflets in 2–3 pairs on a stalk, appear very early. Tiny, fragrant, creamy flowers, in late spring, in flat-topped clusters (p.252). Clusters of small, black edible elderberries on red stalks.

CHUSAN PALM *Trachycarpus fortunei*

A Chinese species that is the only true palm to be reliably hardy outdoors in Britain and Ireland. Even then it is restricted to milder areas and sometimes requires frost protection in hard winters.

AKA Chinese Windmill Palm, Chinese Fan Palm.

Height 10 m.

Range Coastal areas of S and W Britain. More widespread in Ireland.

ID Radiating fans of fronds on top of a single, straight trunk. Each fan is about 1 m across, made up of about 50 deep green sword-like leaflets, each folded down the middle and serrated on both edges. Flower orange first, then yellow in drooping tassels. Blue-black berry-like fruit.

CABBAGE PALM *Cordyline australis*

This New Zealand native is related to the agaves, and is therefore not a true palm. It is very distinctive with its massive central plume, and is often surrounded by root suckers. In Britain, outside palm houses and large conservatories, it is mainly restricted to seaside towns in the south and west, where it is often grown in municipal parks. In Ireland it is much commoner and is found in front gardens in towns and villages. There are ornamental varieties with coloured leaves.

AKA Cabbage Tree.

Height 10 m.

Range Seaside towns on milder British coasts, more widespread in Ireland.

ID Unmistakable straight stem ending in a large, symmetrical plume of strong, sharp, lance-like leaves, 60–90 cm long. Small cream-white, fragrant flower on huge stem, branching out of the leaf plume. Small blue-white berry.

OTHER PALMS

Apart from the Chusan Palm (p.229) and the palm-like Cabbage Palm (p.230), no similar trees are reliably hardy outdoors in Britain and Ireland. However, there are two other palms that are very commonly found further south in Europe and occasionally grow indoors or with some form of shelter in milder parts of Britain.

Date Palm, *Phoenix dactylifera* (**below**), is an important commercial plant over most of its range, which includes Sicily and parts of Spain, and is common as a street ornamental all over southern Europe. The oasis palm, it has long (3–5 m) curving fronds arching out from the top of a single trunk.

Canary Islands Palm, *P. canariensis*, is a smaller, stouter version of the Date Palm from the Canary Islands with brighter green foliage. It has little commercial use, but is a very common ornamental in frost-free places.

TREE DETAILS

Ginkgo fruit (see p. 41)

Wellingtonia bark (see p. 58)

Cedar of Lebanon cones (see p. 68)

White Poplar young female catkins (see p. 90)

TREE DETAILS

Aspen male catkins (see p. 92)

Black Poplar male catkins (see p. 93)

Goat Willow male catkins ('Pussy Willow') (see p. 97)

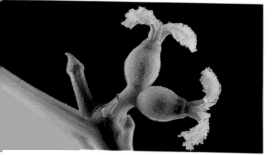

Common Walnut female flowers (see p. 110)

Common Walnut nuts (see p. 110)

Hornbeam catkins (see p. 117)

Hazel male catkins and female flowers (see p. 119)

Turkish Hazel nut (see p. 120)

Tree Details

Persian Ironwood blossom (see p. 150)

London Plane blossom (see p. 151)

Hawthorn blossom (see p. 153)

Medlar blossom (see p. 155)

Rowan blossom (see p. 156)

Wild Service blossom (see p. 159)

Whitebeam blossom (see p. 160)

Blackthorn blossom (see p. 173)

Tree Details

Victoria Plum blossom (see p. 174)

Almond blossom (see p. 176)

Apricot blossom (see p. 177)

Peach blossom (see p. 178)

TREE DETAILS

Cherry Laurel blossom (see p. 183)

Portugal Laurel blossom (see p. 184)

Tree Details

Honey Locust spines (see p. 191)

Paper Bark Maple bark (see p. 201)

Horse Chestnut blossom (see p. 205)

Horse Chestnut buds (see p. 205)

Spindle fruit (see p. 206)

Buckthorn male flowers (see p. 207)

TREE DETAILS

Small-leaved Lime blossom (see p. 209)

Blue Gum fruit (see p. 216)

Cornelian Cherry blossom (see p. 219)

Ash seeds ('ash-key') (see p. 224)

TREE DETAILS

Manna Ash blossom (see p. 225)

Bean Tree blossom (see p. 227)

TREE DETAILS

Elder blossom (see p. 228)

Index

The first page number given
refers to the main entry for the
species. Page numbers in brackets
refer to pictures only.

254